FABLED FLOWERS

Kumiko Sudo

FABLED FLOWERS

Innovative Quilt Patterns Inspired by Japanese
Sashiko and Origami Traditions

KUMIKO SUDO

 THE QUILT DIGEST PRESS
Simply the Best from NTC Publishing Group
Lincolnwood, Illinois U.S.A.

Editorial and production direction by Anne Knudsen.

Book and cover design by Rick Dinihanian and John Lyle,

     Green Lizard Design, St. Helena, CA.

Technical Editing by Randi Nervig and Kandy Petersen.

Technical Drawings by Kandy Petersen.

Introduction edited by Mary Elizabeth Johnson.

Photography by Sharon Risedorph, San Francisco.

Origami samples by Marie Griswold, age 14.

Printed in Hong Kong

Library of Congress Cataloging-in-Publication Data

Sudo, Kumiko

Fabled Flowers: innovative quilt patterns inspired by Japanese sashiko and

origami traditions / Kumiko Sudo. — 1st ed.

    p. cm.

  ISBN: 0-8442-2645-9

  1. Quilting—Patterns. 2. Appliqué—Patterns. 3. Sashiko. 4. Flowers in art.

  5. Origami. I. Title

  TT835.S79 1996

  746.37—dc20   94-35649

                     CIP

Published by The Quilt Digest Press,

a division of NTC Publishing Group,

4255 West Touhy Avenue,

Lincolnwood (Chicago), Illinois 60646-1975, U.S.A.

A Season for Thistles
A Fable by Kumiko Sudo

It is late spring on the prairie and huge thistles are blooming everywhere, their soft figures like brush puffs. It seems that they are waiting for the summer just ahead of them, as they swing their heavy heads comfortably in the waves of the breeze.

From the top of the hill, I am filled with joy as I watch the panorama of thistles, grasses, hawks flying, deer, and squirrels playing. As the hot summer sunset falls, I visualize the thistles changing their dress into light gray cotton balls of winged seeds. All change at once, readying themselves for the journey they will take on the breeze that arrives far from the sea.

Hundreds and thousands of seeds leap up into the sky and fly away. The little children chase them and try to put them on their palms, yet the seed puffs still go on their journey.

As the maple trees change their colors into yellow, orange, and red from the proud summer green, the thistle seeds choose where they wish to land.

Squirrels busily gather acorns and hide them under the ground. The gray hares are busy as well.

Oak leaves fall on the ground, covering up the thistle seeds like warm brown blankets. The cold north wind blows over the branches, now clad in light green moss.

The coats of the deer change from caramel to brown as the sky turns from gray to black and brings snow. The deer no longer come into my garden.

I devote myself to my design work. The snowfall matches my heartbeat as I watch it through my studio window. My dog, beside my desk, watches the snow flakes get bigger and bigger. The hills turn white. He wants to run in the newly fallen snow.

Waking in the mid-afternoon, I feel spring is almost here.

The thistle seeds, after many long winter months under the warm ground, peek out with their creamy yellow buds, looking eagerly for the spring sunlight.

The flower season has come again. Those bright thistles start blooming. Yes, the beautiful and fragrant spring has arrived.

Quietly the breeze passes by and opens the door to my flower garden.

CONTENTS

❖ Indicates assembly instructions for full quilt.

INTRODUCTION

For as long as I remember, storytelling has been a part of my life. When I was five years old, my sister, who was eight, made for me a six-page picture book illustrating one of Aesop's fables. It was a story about the son of a miller, a donkey, and a flour mill. So enchanted was I with the gift that I showed it to several of our neighbors. As I leafed through the pages, my sister would tell the story. This is one of my earliest childhood memories. It is from my sister that I first learned the joy of storytelling.

Fantasies and fables are still, for me, an important part of the creative process. As I designed my *Fabled Flowers* blocks, my imagination was fired by stories I remembered and others that I dreamed up as I worked. My memories of childhood are filled with stories that continue to inspire me. I remember the bonsai tended lovingly by my father. Those miniature pine, maple, apple, and plum trees created a small wilderness, complete with a forest floor of dark green moss. Oh, the stories that danced in my head and the creatures and flowers I saw as I gazed into that magical bonsai garden! Once, as a going-away gift when I left home to spend some time with my aunt, my father gave me one of his favorite bonsai. During the journey, the dish in which he had carefully planted it was broken. I replanted the tiny bonsai in the ground outside my aunt's home, and, in just a few months, it grew into a large tree, its branches towering above me. So many stories came to life for me as I watched that tree grow!

Movies, too, fed my childhood fantasies. I loved Walt Disney's famous cast of characters–Donald Duck, Mickey Mouse, Dumbo, and many, many others. As young as I was, I was able to observe the influence that nature had on Disney's own fantasies. A scene I remember with happiness is one in which a green moth sings as he dances across the keys of a piano. I remember best the beautiful flowers in the background, especially the tulips, their lips painted with lipstick as they sang and danced.

When I was eight years old, my life changed dramatically. I moved from the bustling city of Tokyo to the suburbs of Kamakura to live with my aunt. This was the beginning of a new life, a life filled with the sights and sounds of nature in the quiet, forested mountains of Kamakura. Each day as I walked home from school through ancient woodland that was the site of a one-thousand-year-old Shinto shrine, I absorbed the wonders of nature, the plants, the flowers, the fallen leaves. I remember spending an entire morning just watching a tiny ant, fascinated by his busy-work. One of my favorite pastimes, enjoyed by children the world over, was collecting insects. I especially liked capturing flying insects in my butterfly net and putting them in my little bamboo insect cage.

My aunt and uncle opened new vistas for me through their hobby of collecting and pressing alpine flowers. They kept the flower collection in their library, with another treasure, their stamp collection. Flowers and insects from around the world colorfully decorated the faces of hundreds of stamps. Many happy after-school hours were spent in that library studying those collections.

I think of those early years as the first page in my creative life. The colors, the textures, the patterns, and the simple beauty of nature taught me the essentials of design and remain the source of my inspiration.

A Child's Notes on Nature

During the time I lived in Kamakura, I began to keep notebooks of my thoughts to share with my mother when she visited. I still have those notebooks and would like to share some of my earliest and most innocent observations with you. As a child, these thoughts would inspire me to make up gentle fables about the flowers and the creatures of the forest. I do the same today and the joy I feel in the stories becomes part of my work and adds a special texture to the quilts I design.

❖ A gust of spring breeze passes my cheek and goes quietly through my heart, leaving behind the green color of new buds.

❖ Waking up from a deep sleep, gently my heart enters a bed of flowers.

❖ One blossom seduces me into the entire, wondrous world of flowers.

❖ Who taught the flowers to form so beautifully in perfect geometrical patterns?

❖ A flower of half-an-inch blooms humbly, uttering no words in this great universe.

❖ I wish all flowers could bloom forever.

❖ Suddenly comes a hummingbird with its long beak and shiny green and blue feathers to sip honey. Its wings hum vigorously, like a helicopter. The hummingbird has no word of gratitude. The flower keeps the silence also.

❖ The threads I removed from some kimonos yesterday are dancing around the garden in the wind. I see some little birds gathering the threads to make their nests. Later, I sprinkle fragments of fabric around and watch the same tiny birds come down and pick them up as though they had found a treasure.

❖ The red sunlight, the blue sky, the green trees, the brown soil, the colorful flowers, bugs, animals, and we people all come from the same place and live under heaven.

Today, as I work in my studio to bring to life the designs within these pages, the beauty of nature is my constant inspiration. When I need a fresh approach, I slip away to spend time in my flower garden. I water my old friends, the flowers that have been with me throughout the summer. I make beds for new friends, those I discover during one of my frequent trips to local nurseries. As I happily tend my flowers, I reminisce on those wondrous flowers of my childhood in Japan. My head filled with new ideas--lines, fabrics, and colors--I go back into my studio, taking the fragrance of the flowers with me.

I learn from nature as it unfolds before me. Flowers bloom but briefly. The images I create in fabric are my attempt to prolong that short, sweet life

希望の花

Kumiko Sudo

ORIGAMI: FROM FABRIC TO PAPER TO FABRIC?

The craft of *origami*, or folding objects out of paper without cutting, gluing, or decorating, is so familiar to the Japanese that they consider it an integral aspect of their culture, rather than as an art form. The origins of the word indicate just how ingrained the craft is in Japanese culture: *ori* means "to fold," and *kami*, which becomes *gami* when combined with *ori*, means "paper" and also "God."

The very early history of *origami* remains veiled in obscurity. Some sources claim that it could not have preceded the invention of paper about two thousand years ago, but an alternative theory is far more intriguing to fabric artists: some authorities say that paper-folding is derived from an older art of folding cloth. If that is the case, then Kumiko Sudo has revived a truly ancient, and lost, technique when she folds fabric into three-dimensional flowers. Although nothing is known of the art of early fabric-folding, we might legitimately assume that those extinct techniques were the predecessors of present-day origami.

The classic folds of origami divide into two categories. There are those used to make small folded tokens, known as *noshi*, that are attached to gifts. *Noshi* are a holdover from ceremonial wrappers (*tsutsumi*) that were used to wrap gifts, especially of flowers; each type of flower had its own special fold.

The other classic form of origami is more familiar: it is the folding of paper to make three-dimensional objects, such as fish, birds, animals, furniture, flowers, insects, and human figures. Many of these objects contain amusing action features: a bird flaps its wings when the tail is pulled, or a frog jumps when tapped on the back.

The greatest of contemporary paper-folders is considered to be Akira Yoshizawa of Tokyo. He has written several books on origami, and has originated a large number of new, often fantastically complex, figures possessing great realism and beauty. He is credited with bringing a whole new era of creativity to the medium and remains the dominant force in the art in Japan, where new forms are constantly evolving.

It was not until the 1950s that the gentle art of origami found popularity in the West, although it had flourished in Spain and in South America as early as the turn of the century. Paper-folding was demonstrated on television for the first time in 1956 by Robert Harbin, a British master magician who earned real fame through his interest in origami and his book, *Paper Magic.*

Kumiko Sudo certainly agrees that there is real magic in origami, as she creates her three-dimensional designs out of nothing but folds. But Kumiko has changed the medium, and now uses fabric, rather than the paper of her youth. In *Fabled Flowers*, she has skillfully transferred those techniques that come to her as naturally as breathing to a new material, and the results enrich us all.

Fabric Origami

Anyone who has practiced elaborate napkin folding to make such designs as the Bishop's mitre or the buffet fold has used the techniques of origami. If, however, even this basic experience is beyond your acquaintance, do not worry. With Kumiko as your guide, you will find the techniques easy to learn. Here are a few points to remember as you work.

❖ Study each of Kumiko's folding diagrams carefully before you begin. Determine which is the right and wrong side of the fabric. Go through the step-by-step instructions mentally before you even pick up the fabric. You may find it helpful to practice each new shape on a sample so that you solve any difficulties before you begin on your final piece.

❖ Cut out all fabric templates with care so that the measurements are exact. Transfer all markings that indicate where folds are to be made.

❖ Always fold accurately and neatly.

❖ Crease each fold firmly with the back of your thumbnail. Good creases make the folding easier, and they serve as guides to future steps.

❖ One difference between folding paper and folding fabric is that paper is available with different colors on the two sides. To achieve the same effect when folding fabric, you must first sew the two colors of your choice together, then turn them right side out and press. Often finger-pressing will be adequate.

You will find that the same procedures are used over and over again. You will soon come so proficient with them that you, like Kumiko, can carry them out almost without thinking.

SASHIKO: DECORATIVE QUILTING

There are those that would take the position that all quilting is decorative, but the patterns of sashiko are more circumscribed than those of Western quilting. This traditional Japanese folkcraft began as a mending method wherein multiple rows of stitching were used to attach a second layer of fabric over the worn areas of work clothes. During the time when most fabrics were of home manufacture, before mass production of fabric was a given, sashiko was a valued technique for fastening together multiple layers of fabrics. Old fabrics could then be recycled as a whole piece, rather than going to the rag bag. The interesting texture added by the sashiko stitches–the word literally means "little stabs"–was a bonus.

Originally, very simple stitches were made in straight lines across the area to be reinforced, but as the decorative possibilities of the technique became apparent, more elaborate stitches were devised. Sashiko stitching was a common sight on peasant and fishermen's work garments until recent times in rural Japan, and even in urban areas, intricate sashiko work can sometimes still be seen on firemen's garments. It is used today as reinforcement stitching for garments worn in the martial arts.

Like the English word *quilt*, the term *sashiko* is used in several different ways. Originally, the word was used to describe garments made of one or more layers of indigo-dyed fabric that had been quilted in various patterns for the purpose of mending, reinforcement, warmth, or decoration. The term has also been applied to a style of weaving done in imitation of this stitching.

Over time, each region of Japan has developed its own distinct sashiko designs. The Shonai in the coastal areas of the Yamagata prefecture, as well as the Sanin in the Kyoto, Hyogo, Tottori, and Shimane prefectures, used the original term *sashiko* to describe their regional style. Here, the stitching runs in all directions over the fabric, attaching two layers so that the front and reverse sides show the same patterns. The simplest pattern consists of tiny parallel running stitches that create dots over the entire garment. Straight and curved stitches are combined to make traditional designs such as persimmon flowers, measuring-boxes, hemp leaves, lozenges, tortoise shells, waves, and so on.

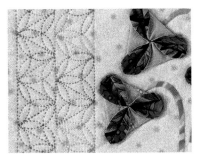

In the western half of the Aomori prefecture, the Tsugaru chose the name *kogin* to describe their unique style of sashiko quilting. In *kogin* stitching, which runs only parallel to the weft, from selvage to selvage, dark blue was combined with white, and the tones were reversed on the front and back of the fabric. About 50 commonly used basic motifs from nature and daily life (plum blossoms, bamboo joints, etc.) have been developed.

A third type of sashiko quilting is from the Nambu, in the north portion of the Iwate prefecture and the eastern half of the Aomori prefecture. It is named *hishizashi*, and it also runs parallel to the weft of the fabric. Traditionally, white or black thread was stitched on pale blue fabric in a pattern of lozenges; later, colored woolen yarns were used. *Hishizashi* has a uniquely colorful and gay appearance compared to the subdued and elegant *kogin*.

Kumiko Sudo has drawn from all regions to produce the exquisite sashiko designs that accompany each of the flowers that follow. The designer's skill is evident in the way she suggests that the stitching of sashiko be used to accent the folded flower designs. The delicate stitching seems somehow to suggest a cloud, or a perhaps a breeze, or maybe even the air through which a butterfly has moved. Surely Kumiko's combinations of origami and sashiko have resulted in some of the loveliest quilt designs ever imagined.

How to Use This Book

In This Book You Will Find

Thirty block designs including:
❖ a color photograph and diagram of each block
❖ step-by-step diagrams for making each block
❖ pattern templates for each block
❖ a sashiko design for each block

Six quilt designs including:
❖ a color photo of each quilt
❖ a color photo and diagram of each pattern block
❖ fabric requirements for blocks and border

A total of thirty new designs, each incorporating fabric origami and sashiko, will inspire, excite, and delight you.

Where to Begin

If you have made quilts from Kumiko Sudo's books *East Quilts West* and *East Quilts West II*, you will already be familiar with the format of this book. If you are new to Kumiko's work, you will immediately notice that *Fabled Flowers* is not like other quilting books. The designs, the colors, the fabrics all come together in a unique blending of Eastern and Western cultures. As you are reading, why not try to create an atmosphere that will help you understand a little more about Kumiko's cultural heritage? Play some Japanese music in the background. Sip a cup of green tea. If you have never had sushi, now may be the perfect time to try it. Take out some decorative paper and experiment with origami. All of these suggestions can help you feel at ease and enter into the spirit of Kumiko's quilts.

In the past, Kumiko used silk from old Japanese garments to make quilts. In this book, she uses contemporary American fabrics. Yet in many cases, the overall effect still reflects a Japanese sensibility. Since the fabrics are available in the United States, you can probably duplicate Kumiko's choices. However, Kumiko feels that color is an individual expression, and her selections are intended for inspiration, not for instruction. In Japan, certain colors and design patterns have symbolic meaning. This is just one way in which Kumiko's cultural heritage has influenced her work, giving her quilts their unique character. You can use *Fabled Flowers* to make a "Kumiko quilt," or you can use your own color and fabric combinations to create one that has your own individual imprint on it.

Some of the designs in *Fabled Flowers* may look puzzling at first, almost off-balance, as if the blocks were cut up and tossed around. In addition, the three-dimensional effect of fabric origami looks a good deal more complex than it is. The fabric, color, and pattern combinations are like nothing we've ever seen before. But as you study them, their own unique beauty, harmony, subtlety, and simplicity becomes clear.

Pointers on Technique

Fabled Flowers differs from other quilting books not only in design and spirit, but in technical matters, too. To ensure successful and enjoyable quilt making, keep these points in mind.

❖ *Fabled Flowers* is intended for those with at least basic skills in sewing and quilting. If you are new to quilting, first familiarize yourself through a book such as *Quilts! Quilts!! Quilts!!!* by Diana McClun and Laura Nownes (The Quilt Digest Press).

❖ Experienced quilters should find the thirty block designs easy to make. Six of the designs include instructions for making full quilts. Beginners should start with one of these to familiarize themselves with Kumiko's methods of sewing and assembly. Then you can go on to make other blocks more easily, comfortably, and confidently.

❖ Most of the flower designs involve sewing curved seams. For perfect curved seams, Kumiko prefers to use a form of appliqué. Her technique involves placing a fabric piece, with the seam allowance folded under, on top of the other pieces; the fold is placed along the seamline of the lower piece and blind-stitched by hand. In the instructions, this is what is meant by the term *appliqué* for curved seams. The term *sew* indicates a more traditional method of sewing the pieces together, right sides facing, using a running stitch on the wrong side of the seamline. Straight seams are sewn this way, and you may use hand or machine stitching. Kumiko stitches everything–curved and straight–by hand. Although the results are excellent when sewn by machine, Kumiko prefers to sew by hand, as she feels that the hand is directed not only by the eye but by the heart. The machine puts a distance between her and her work.

❖ The fabric charts may seem to specify an overly generous amount of fabric. This is because curved pieces take up more space and result in more waste than straight-line templates. Also, it is far better to have a bit too much fabric than too little.

❖ The fabric requirements for borders on the quilts are figured without piecing if they are over 2" (5cm) wide. Narrower borders are figured to be pieced, to save fabric. Of courses, the decision to piece or not to piece is up to you. Sometimes the border is of one of the fabrics that appear in the block; in this case, you may want to use the waste fabric from the border to make the block pieces.

❖ Full-size templates for all blocks are provided at the back of the book. All templates and measurements include a ¼" (6mm) seam allowance, unless otherwise indicated.

❖ Instructions are given for making block and quilt tops only. To finish your project, you will need to buy batting and backing fabric, assemble the layers, and quilt them together. Kumiko considers quilting to be an accent, "rather than something to be seen all over the picture." In quilts used as wall hangings such accent stitching will suffice; however, quilts used as bedding will require more extensive quilting. Kumiko seldom draws a design, but usually quilts freestyle. She rarely uses thread to match the fabric--for example, she often uses purple thread for yellow fabric, and green for blue fabric--and may use two or three different thread colors in one quilt.

❖ Experiment. Use your imagination. You may want to make a whole quilt or make several individual blocks in different designs. The generous block size makes them ideal for small wall hangings, pillows, or other projects. You can also add to or subtract from the width and number of borders to get a variety of effects and a variety of sizes.

A CORNFLOWER NAMED KORORO *grew alongside a country path. One*
with thirst, she wished and wished for water. Then, a young girl
picked her up, and took her home. There, she laid Kororo on the kitchen
Kororo became thirstier and thirstier. To make matters worse, the family
Kororo a terrible fright to see the cat's nose so close. Scared and thirsty, Koro
girl's mother saw her there and put her in a crystal vase filled with water.
vase was the best place in the world to be and wanted to make everyone arou

M A K I N G   T H E   B L O C K

1. Cut two complementary pieces of fabric, 15 ½" x 15"
   (39cm x 38cm) and 4 ½" x 15" (11cm x 38cm).
   Sew them together to make the background square.
   This includes a ½" (13mm) seam allowance.
2. Using the templates on pages 92 and 93, lightly draw
   the outlines of the pattern onto the background square.
3. Copy the sashiko design from page 76 onto the
   background square.
4. Cut a 19" x 15" (48cm x 38cm) piece of cotton or
   polyester batting. Baste it to the back of the background square.
5. Complete the sashiko as shown on the sashiko design.
6. Using the templates on pages 92 and 93, cut out all
   pieces. Add a ⅛" (3mm) seam allowance.
7. Appliqué in this order, leaves A and B, leaves C and
   D, leaves F, H, and I, and leaves K and L.
8. Appliqué in this order, stems E, G, J, and M.

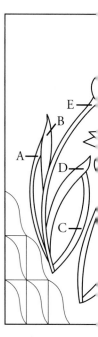

1.

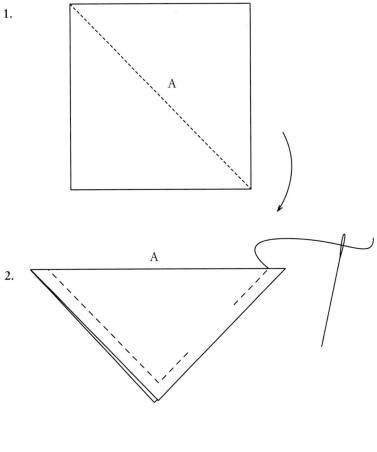

2.

1. Fold all fourteen N pieces diagonally along dotted line A, right sides together, as shown in illustration 1.
2. Sew raw edges together, leaving an opening for turning, as in illustration 2. Turn right side out. Blind stitch the opening. Finger press the seams.
3. Fold again, slightly off-center, along dotted line B. Press. You will now have four folded triangle petals for each large flower and two for the small flower. See illustrations 3, 4, and 5.
4. Appliqué four petals onto the background square for each of the three large flowers, overlapping them a little, as shown in the block photograph.
5. For each of the three large flowers, appliqué piece O over the petals, stuffing with a piece of cotton, as in illustration 6.
6. Appliqué two petals onto the background square for the small flower. Appliqué piece P over the petals, stuffing with a piece of cotton.

3.

4.

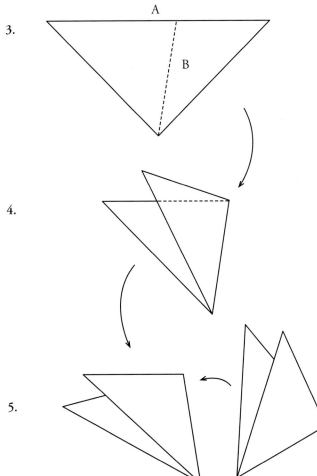

5.

6.

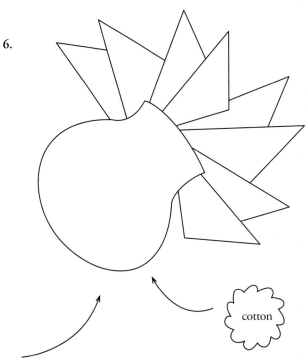

cotton

*A*S YOU KNOW, *crickets always make music at night, and Mr. Grasshopper's friend the cricket was no exception. All night long, he played beautiful music on the violin, keeping Mr. Grasshopper awake. Mr. Grasshopper decided that, since he couldn't sleep, it would be a good idea if he could learn to make beautiful music, too. So one day he went to visit his aunt, Teru, who lived in a small village nearby and told her his wish. Teru told him to talk to the morning glory flowers that grew on her backyard fence. Mr. Grasshopper was clever—he knew that flowers like water, so he carried a bucket of water with him when he went to see the morning glory. After meeting all the flowers, he agreed to exchange the bucket of water for a beautiful gold blossom. That morning glory blossom became Mr. Grasshopper's new trumpet. From that moment on, day or night, no one got much sleep, but the forest was filled with beautiful music.*

MAKING THE BLOCK

1. Cut two pieces of complementary fabric, 15" x 12 ½" (38cm x 32cm) and 15" x 3 ½" (38cm x 9cm). Sew them together to make the background square. This includes a ½" (13mm) seam allowance.
2. Using the templates on pages 93 and 94, lightly draw the outlines of the pattern onto the background square.
3. Copy the sashiko design from page 76 onto the background square.
4. Cut a 15" x 15" (38cm x 38cm) piece of cotton or polyester batting. Baste it to the back of the background square.
5. Complete the sashiko as shown on the sashiko design.
6. Using the templates on pages 93 and 94, cut out all pattern pieces. Add a ⅛" (3mm) seam allowance.
7. Appliqué support poles A and B.
8. Appliqué leaves C and D and quilt along the lines drawn on the patterns.
9. Appliqué two E pieces.

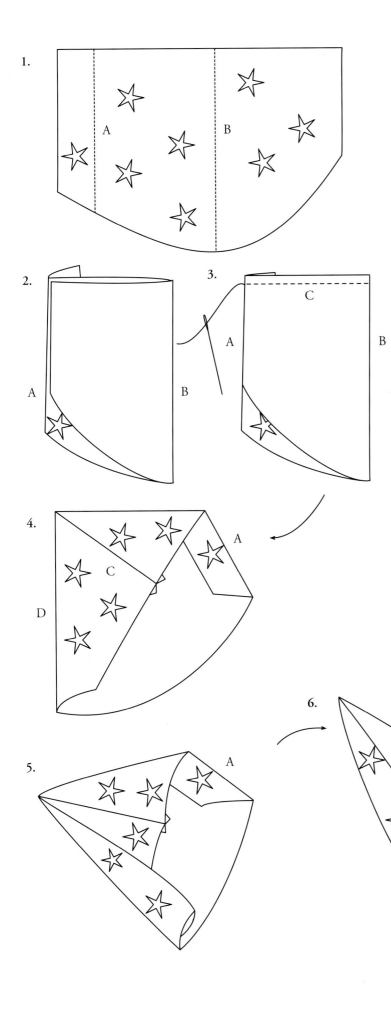

MAKING THE FLOWERS
Make 3
Two of the flowers are open; the third is closed.

1. Sew two F pieces, right sides together. Leave an opening. Turn right side out through the opening and blind stitch it closed. Stitch along the dotted line as shown on the pattern and gather slightly. Attach this petal F on top of one of the E petals on the background square. Repeat this step for the other petal E.

2. Sew together two F pieces as before. Turn right side out. Fold petal into thirds. Stitch calyx H at base to make a partially blooming flower. Sew onto the background square.

3. Using three-ply embroidery floss and outline stitch, embroider the vines onto the background square.

4. Sew the completed flowers onto the background square.

MAKING THE BUDS
Make 3

1. Fold piece G along dotted lines A and B, as shown in illustrations 1 and 2.

2. Sew through all three layers of fabric along line C. Turn right side out. See illustrations 3 and 4.

3. Roll the edge of corner D towards corner A until they meet, as in illustrations 5 and 6.

4. Sew the rolled material together at the bottom. Wrap calyx H around the bottom of the bud. See illustrations 7 and 8.

5. Sew the completed buds onto the background square.

*T*HERE ONCE WAS *a cricket named Kika who played a violin given to him by his father. Kika was not happy with the sound of his violin, so he decided to buy a new one. When spring came, he floated down the river on a camellia flower to the nearest village. He went into a shop where violins were made. There, he saw a tall cricket wearing a fancy black silk hat who was in the middle of buying the best violin in the shop. The elegant cricket was Kika's father, who, to Kika's great surprise, was buying the beautiful new violin as a special gift for his son.*

MAKING THE BLOCK

1. Cut a background square using templates A, B, and C on page 95 and sew them together. This includes a ½" (13mm) seam allowance.
2. Using the rest of the templates on pages 95 to 97, lightly draw the outlines of the pattern onto the background square.
3. Copy the sashiko design from page 77 onto the background square.
4. Cut a 17" x 17" (43cm x 43cm) piece of cotton or polyester batting. Baste it to the back of the background square.
5. Complete the sashiko as shown on the sashiko design.
6. Using the templates on pages 95 to 97, cut out all pattern pieces from selected fabrics. Add a ⅛" (3mm) seam allowance.
7. Appliqué leaves D, E, and F.
8. Appliqué branches G, H, and I.

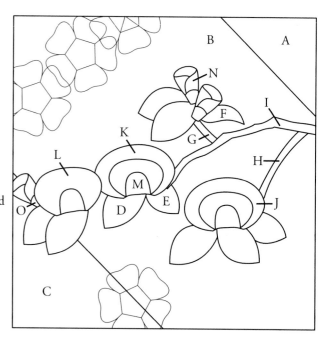

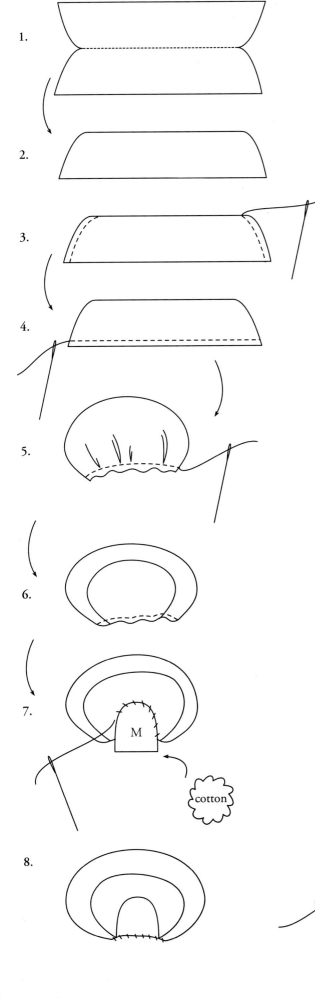

1.

2.

3.

4.

5.

6.

7.

8.

MAKING THE FLOWERS
Make 3
For the first flower, use pieces J, L, and M. For the second, use pieces K, L, and M. For the third, use pieces L and M only.

1. For each flower, fold largest petal along the dotted line, right sides together, as shown in illustrations 1 and 2.

2. Sew the right and left sides, as in illustration 3. Turn right side out. Finger press seams.

3. Take a running stitch along the bottom and gather, as in illustrations 4 and 5. Be sure to catch both layers as you stitch.

4. Prepare the next petal in the same way and sew the two pieces together, as in illustration 6. Sew the flower onto the background square. Leave the bottom unstitched.

5. Appliqué piece M to the center of the flower, using a little cotton as stuffing. Tuck the straight edge of piece M under the larger petals. Appliqué across the bottom of all three pieces, as shown in illustrations 7 and 8.

6. Sew the remaining flowers onto the background square.

MAKING THE BUDS
Make 3

1. Sew two N pieces, right sides together, as shown in illustration 9. Turn right side out. Finger press seam.

2. Fold in thirds. Stitch along bottom straight edge. See illustrations 10, 11, and 12.

3. Sew two O pieces, right sides together, as in illustration 13. Turn right side out. Finger press seam.

4. Wrap piece O around piece N. Stitch in place. Tuck bottom of piece O under piece N. The completed bud in shown in illustration 14.

5. Sew the completed buds onto the background square.

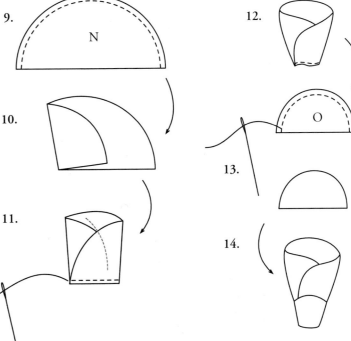

9.

10.

11.

12.

13.

14.

cotton

N

M

O

*T*HERE ONCE WAS *a caterpillar named Taro whose favorite hobby was climbing tall flowers. One day he decided to climb a dyer's grape that grew nearby—the tallest flower he could see. He thought of it as a challenge. As he slowly climbed up the green leaves, Taro enjoyed the warm breezes blowing across his face. When he reached the top, he rested among the beautiful flowers and looked out over the beautiful world as far as his eye could see. "What a wonderful place this is!" he thought. His deepest wish was that someday, in a different life, he would be able to return and thank the flowers again for giving him this opportunity to see so much of the world.*

MAKING THE BLOCK

1. Cut a background square 15" x 15" (38cm x 38cm). This includes a ½" (13mm) seam allowance.
2. Using the templates on pages 98 and 99, lightly draw the outlines of the pattern onto the background square.
3. The sashiko design is free-form. Copy it onto the background square using the diagram opposite as a guide.
4. Cut a 15" x 15" (38cm x 38cm) piece of cotton or polyester batting. Baste it to the back of the background square.
5. Complete the sashiko as shown on the diagram.
6. Using the templates on pages 98 and 99, cut out all pieces. Add a ⅛" (3mm) seam allowance.
7. Appliqué in this order leaves A, B, and C, leaves D and E, and leaves F and G.
8. Appliqué stems H and I.
9. Appliqué leaf J with stem K.
10. Appliqué leaves L, M, and N.

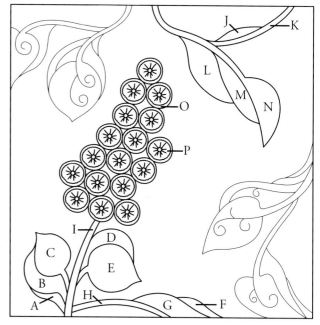

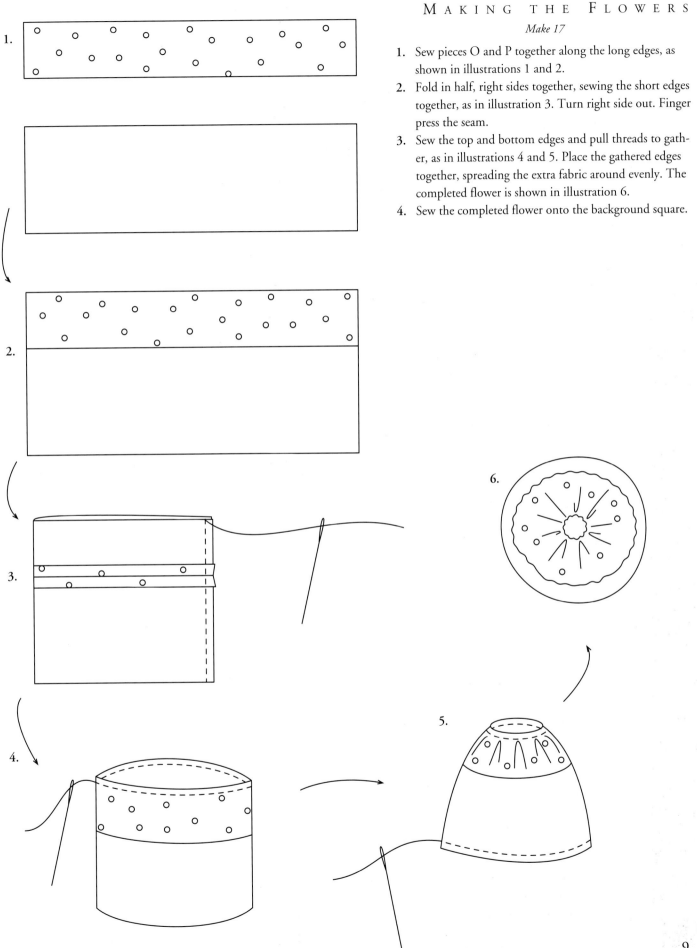

1. Sew pieces O and P together along the long edges, as shown in illustrations 1 and 2.

2. Fold in half, right sides together, sewing the short edges together, as in illustration 3. Turn right side out. Finger press the seam.

3. Sew the top and bottom edges and pull threads to gather, as in illustrations 4 and 5. Place the gathered edges together, spreading the extra fabric around evenly. The completed flower is shown in illustration 6.

4. Sew the completed flower onto the background square.

9

*T*HE RED FUCHSIA *and the humming bird were good friends, always together. In the forest, the lonely bluebell thought how nice it would be if she had a friend like the humming bird, too. One day, a blue jay stopped to talk to the bluebell. She was unhappy because although everyone in the forest admired her beautiful blue feathers, her loud voice made her unpopular. The bluebell was sympathetic and soon they became friends. In fact, they were such good friends that the next spring, the bluebell watched over the blue jay's nest, taking care of her five beautiful light blue eggs.*

MAKING THE BLOCK

1. Cut a background square 15" x 15" (38cm x 38cm). This includes a ½" (13mm) seam allowance.
2. Using the templates on pages 99 to 101, lightly draw the outlines of the pattern onto the background square.
3. Copy the sashiko pattern from page 77 onto the background square.
4. Cut a 15" x 15" (38cm x 38cm) piece of cotton or polyester batting. Baste it to the back of the background square.
5. Complete the sashiko as shown on the sashiko design.
6. Using the templates on pages 99 to 101, cut out all the pieces from selected fabric. Add a ⅛" (3mm) seam allowance.
7. Appliqué leaves A and B.
8. Appliqué the stems in this order: stems C, D, and E, stems F, G, H, and I, stem J, stems K, L, and M.
9. Appliqué three buds N.

1. Sew two O (P) pieces, right sides together, leaving an opening. Turn the flower right side out through the opening. Blind stitch it closed. Finger press all seams.
2. Lightly draw line A on the flower, as shown in illustration 1. Fold along the line.
3. Lightly draw lines B and C on the flower, as shown in illustration 2. Fold first along line B and then along line C, as shown in illustration 3. The completed flower is shown in illustration 4.
4. Sew the completed flowers onto the background square.

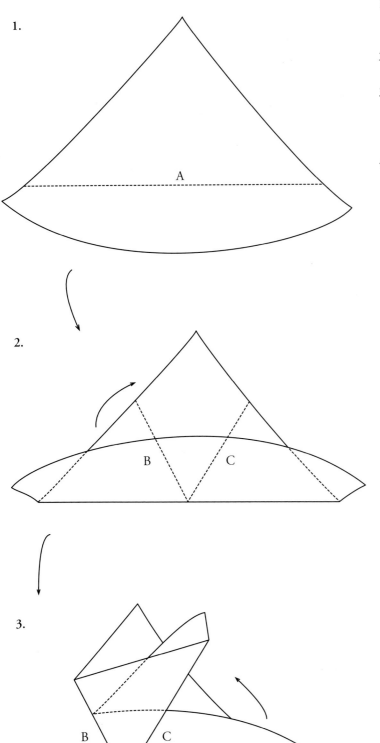

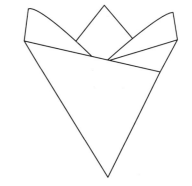

11

Fuchsia Quilt

Quilt Size:
34" x 34" *(86cm x 86cm)*

Block Size:
14" *(36cm)*

Setting:
2 x 2

Blocks:
4

Fabric Needed:

Item	Yards/Cm	
Background	1	*(91)*
Template A	⅛	*(11)*
Template B	⅛	*(11)*
Template C	⅛	*(11)*
Template D	⅛	*(11)*
Template E	⅛	*(11)*
Template F	⅛	*(11)*
Template G	⅛	*(11)*
Template H	⅛	*(11)*
Template I	⅛	*(11)*
Template J	⅛	*(11)*
Template K	⅛	*(11)*
Template L	⅛	*(11)*
Template M	⅛	*(11)*
Template N	⅛	*(11)*
Template O	¾	*(69)*
Template P	½	*(46)*
Border 3" *(76mm)*	⅝	*(57)*

Cutting	Amount
Background and Batting 15" x 15" *(38cm x 38cm)*	4
Template A	24
Template B	12
Template C	4
Template D	4
Template E	4
Template F	4
Template G	4
Template H	4
Template I	4
Template J	4
Template K	4
Template L	4
Template M	4
Template N	12
Template O	24
Template P	16

Border width cut 3 ½" *(89mm)* including ¼" *(6mm)* seam allowance.

Use diagram as guide for assembly.

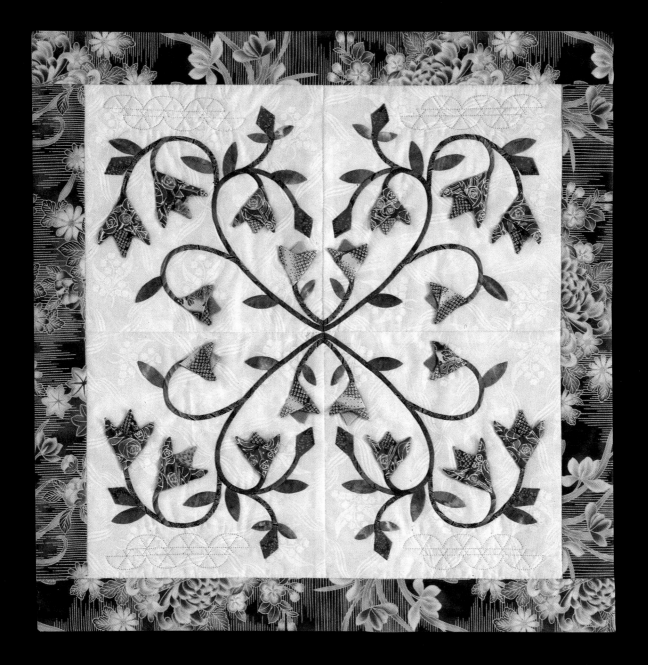

A LITTLE BIRD NAMED *Kurori went to visit her friend who lived in a house with many glass windows. Kurori had never come across windows before, so when she thought she was flying right into the house, she hit the glass instead and fell to the ground unconscious. A dogwood tree in full bloom grew in the garden outside the window. As time went by, the petals from the blossoms began to fall all around Kurori, the sleeping little bird. Their sweet aroma gently awoke her from her long sleep.*

MAKING THE BLOCK

1. Cut a background square 15" x 15" (38cm x 38cm). This includes a ½" (13mm) seam allowance.
2. Using the templates on pages 101 and 102, lightly draw the outline of the design onto the background square.
3. Copy the sashiko design from page 78 onto the background square.
4. Cut a 15" x 15" (38cm x 38cm) piece of cotton or polyester batting. Baste it to the back of the background square.
5. Complete the sashiko as shown on the sashiko design.
6. Using the templates on pages 101 and 102, cut out all pieces from selected fabrics. Add a ⅛" (3mm) seam allowance.
7. Appliqué stems A and B and leaves C, D, and E.
8. Appliqué stems F and G and leaf H.
9. Appliqué stem I, leaf J, stem K, and leaf L.
10. Appliqué stems M, N, O, and P, and leaf Q.

1. Sew two complementary R pieces, right sides together, leave an opening. Turn right side out. Blind stitch closed. Finger press seam.
2. Using a running stitch, sew from A to B, as shown in illustration 1. Pull the thread to gather the fabric and back stitch twice to hold the gathers, as in illustration 2.
3. Repeat, sewing from B to C, from C to D, and from D to A. The completed flower is shown in illustration 3.
4. Fold the tip of each petal down toward the center of the flower and stitch, as in illustration 4.
5. Take a running stitch around the inner circle of piece S. Pull to gather the fabric. Back stitch twice to hold the gathers. Sew onto the center of the flower, as in illustration 5.
6. Sew the completed flowers onto the background square.

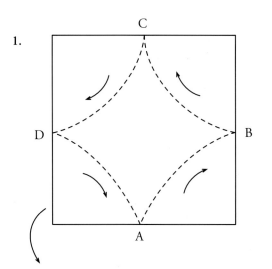

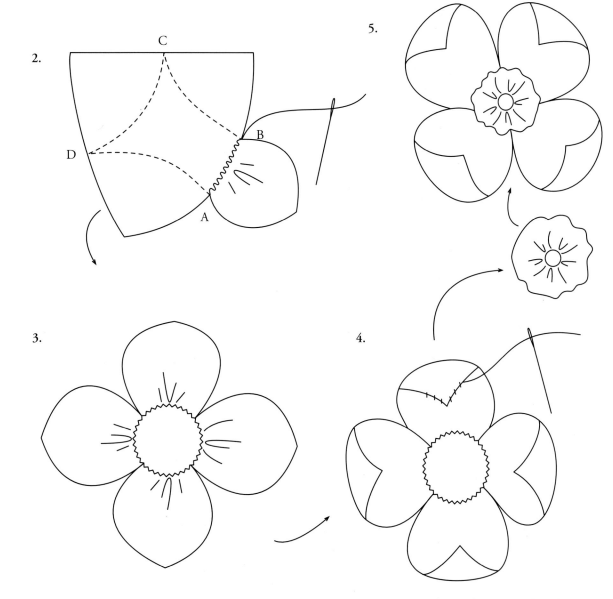

*O*NE FALL DAY, *when the sun made long shadows in the forest, a squirrel lay his blanket on the grass to dry. When he came back later to get it, he was surprised to find a gray rabbit there sleeping. The rabbit awoke with a start and the two looked at each other with big round eyes. Overcoming his surprise, the rabbit ran away, but in his fright, ran smack into a pomegranate tree. Several large, ripe pomegranates fell to the ground. The squirrel was as happy about this gift as the rabbit had been about his nice nap under the warm blanket.*

MAKING THE BLOCK

1. Cut a background square 17" x 17" (43cm x 43cm). This includes a ½" (13mm) seam allowance. Appliqué a curved piece of fabric at the bottom to represent a hill, as shown in the block photograph.
2. Using the templates on page 102, lightly draw the outline of the design onto the background square.
3. Copy the sashiko design from page 78 onto the background square.
4. Cut a 17" x 17" (43cm x 43cm) piece of cotton or polyester batting. Baste it to the back of the background square.
5. Complete the sashiko as shown on the sashiko design.
6. Using the templates on page 102, cut out all pieces from selected fabrics. Add a ⅛" (3mm) seam allowance.
7. Using three-ply embroidery thread and outline stitch, sew the stem lines onto the background square.
8. Appliqué all six leaves A.

1.

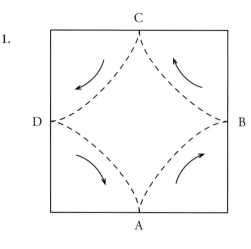

Make 11
Use template B to make four small flowers and
template C to make seven large flowers.

1. Sew two complementary B (C) pieces, right sides together, leave an opening. Turn right side out. Blind stitch closed. Finger press seam.

2. Using a running stitch, sew from A to B, as shown in illustration 1. Pull the thread to gather the fabric and back stitch twice to hold the gathers, as in illustration 2.

3. Repeat, sewing from B to C, from C to D, and from D to A. The completed flower is shown in illustration 3.

4. Stuff a little cotton into the center of the flower. Using a running stitch, sew around the bottom of the petals and gather, as in illustration 4.

5. Sew the flowers onto the background square. Pull one petal of each flower away from the background.

6. Sew and gather six D pieces, as in illustration 5. Sew onto the background square.

2.

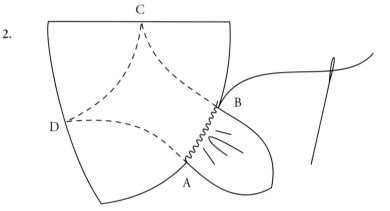

5.

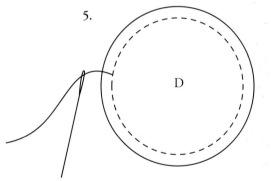

3.

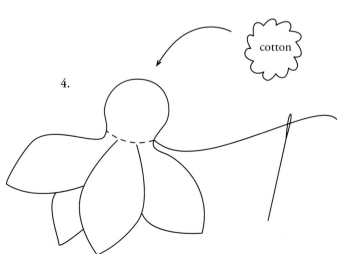

cotton

4.

*T*HE BABY POSSUM *and the baby porcupine were best friends. One day, they overheard their parents talking about a large field of wild strawberries just over the hill and they decided they would like to see it for themselves. When no one was looking, off they went and they filled their little tummies with delicious strawberries. On their way home, a huge deer with big antlers crossed their path and, frightened out of their wits, they ran for cover. The baby porcupine hid in a thistle bush and the baby possum found a hiding place among a cluster of delicate snowdrop flowers. Once the buck had walked by, the two friends scurried home, promising they would never sneak off again.*

MAKING THE BLOCK

1. Cut a background square from templates A and B on page 103 and piece them together. This includes a ½" (13mm) seam allowance.
2. Using the templates on pages 103 and 104, lightly draw the outline of the design onto the background square.
3. The sashiko design is free-form. Copy it onto the background square using the diagram opposite as a guide.
4. Cut a 17" x 17" (43cm x 43cm) piece of cotton or polyester batting. Baste it to the back of the background square.
5. Complete the sashiko as shown on the diagram.
6. Using the templates on pages 103 and 104, cut out all pieces from selected fabrics. Add a 1/8" (3mm) seam allowance.
7. Appliqué stems C, D, E, F, G, and H and leaves I, J, K, and L.
8. Appliqué stem M and leaves N, O, P, and Q.

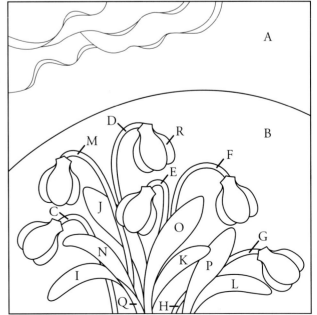

1. Sew together two R pieces, leaving an opening. Turn through the opening and blind stitch it closed. Finger press seams.
2. Fold the center of the flower, as in illustrations 2 and 3.
3. Sew the completed flowers onto the background square.

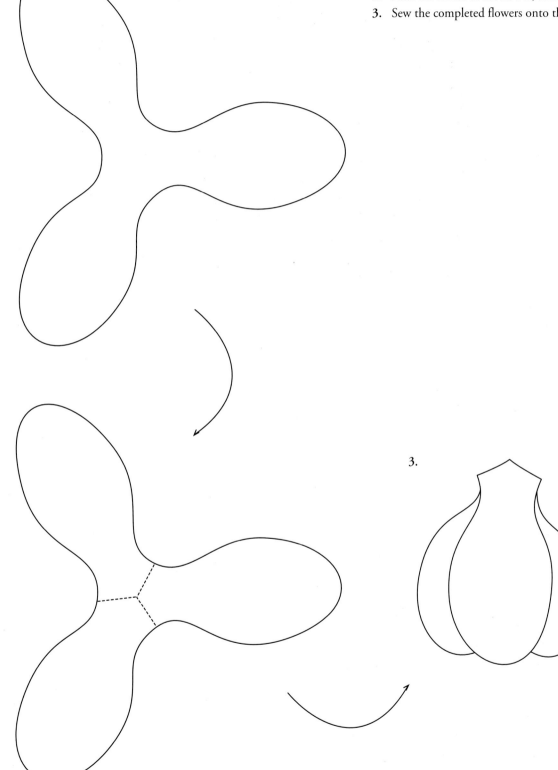

1.

2.

3.

GOLDBUG LOVED TO travel and took every opportunity to see new places. One day, while he was sitting in an oak tree, a young girl wearing a straw hat walked by. She was out on a walk to pick dandelions. Goldbug flew onto the hat and traveled with her. As she reached the dandelion patch and stooped to pick a flower, Goldbug fell from her hat onto an oak leaf. The wind picked up the leaf and blew it into a nearby stream. Goldbug lay back and enjoyed the ride down the creek, amazed at all the new places and new things he saw. He did not know or care where he ended up. He simply looked forward to the new adventures that the next day would bring.

MAKING THE BLOCK

1. Cut a background square 15" x 15" (38cm x 38cm). This includes a ½" (13mm) seam allowance.
2. Using the templates on pages 105 and 106, lightly draw the outline of the design onto the background square.
3. Copy the sashiko design from page 79 onto the background square.
4. Cut a 15" x 15" (38cm x 38cm) piece of cotton or polyester batting. Baste it to the back of the background square.
5. Complete the sashiko as shown on the sashiko design.
6. Using the templates on pages 105 and 106, cut out all pieces from selected fabrics. Add a ⅛" (3mm) seam allowance.
7. Appliqué stem A and leaves B and C.
8. Appliqué stem D, leaf E, and stem F.
9. Appliqué leaves G, H, I, J, K, L, and M.

1. Sew two N pieces, right sides together, leaving an opening. Blind stitch it closed. Finger press seams.
2. Lightly draw a six-pointed star on piece N, as shown in illustration 1.
3. Using a running stitch, sew from A to B. Gather. Back stitch twice to hold the gather in place.
4. Continue in the same way, sewing from B to C, from C to D, from D to E, from E to F, from F to G, from G to H, from H to I, from I to J, from J to K, from K to L, and from L to A. Gather each section as you go. Back stitch twice each time to hold the gathers in place. The completed flower is shown in illustration 2.
5. Sew the completed flowers onto the background square.

*I*N ANCIENT TIMES, *there was a river frog named Karon who lived on the banks of the River Nile in Egypt, where Queen Cleopatra took her baths. Of all the flowers that grew near the river, the queen loved the water lilies most. It was Karon's job to guard the water lilies. The job was handed down through Karon's family from generation to generation. That is why, if you see a frog swimming among the water lilies of the Nile, you'll know its name is Karon.*

Making the Block

1. Cut a background square 15" x 15" (38cm x 38cm). This includes a ½" (13mm) seam allowance.
2. Using the templates on pages 106 to 108, lightly draw the outline of the design onto the background square.
3. Copy the sashiko design from page 79 onto the background square.
4. Cut a 15" x 15" (38cm x 38cm) piece of cotton or polyester batting. Baste it to the back of the background square.
5. Complete the sashiko as shown on the sashiko design.
6. Using the templates on pages 106 to 108, cut out all pieces from selected fabrics. Add a ⅛" (3mm) seam allowance.
7. Appliqué leaves A, B, C, and D.
8. Appliqué stems E and F.
9. Appliqué leaf G and stems H and I.

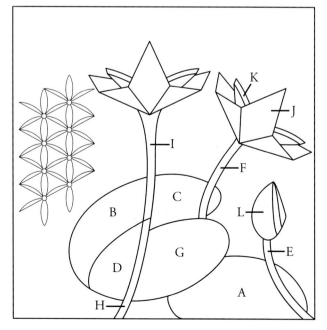

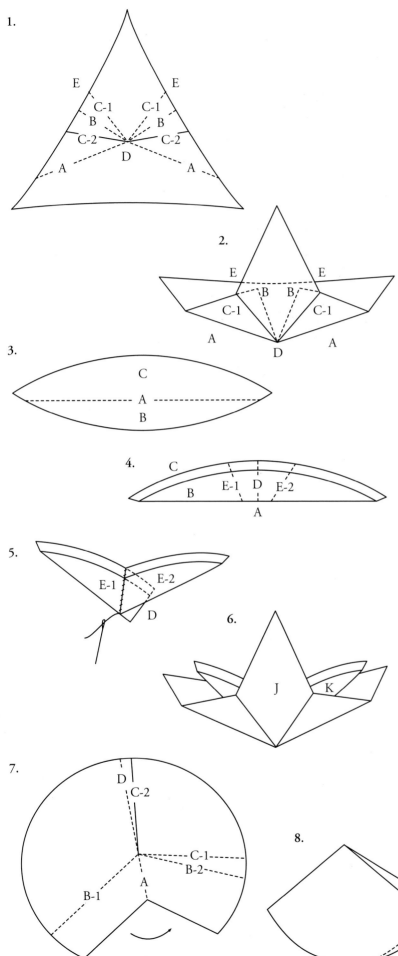

1. Sew two J pieces, right sides together, leaving an opening. Turn right side out through the opening. Blind stitch the opening closed. Finger press the seams.
2. Lightly draw lines A, B, C-1, and C-2 on one side of the fabric, as in illustration 1. The dotted lines A, B, and C-1 are fold lines; C-2 is a guide line.
3. Make the first fold along lines A so that the bottom of the triangle is folded back behind the rest of the triangle.
4. Make the second fold along lines B in the opposite direction. Bring C-1 down to meet C-2, making the third fold along C-1. The completed piece is shown in illustration 2. Note that this piece is not perfectly flat. The ends will bow out a little.
5. Sew two K pieces, right sides together, leaving an opening. Turn right side out through the opening. Blind stitch the opening closed. Finger press the seams.
6. Lightly draw line A on one side of fabric, as shown in illustration 3. Fold along this line, placing the smaller B section on top of the C section.
7. Lightly draw lines D, E-1, and E-2 on the fabric, as in illustration 4. Fold along line D. Bring E-1 to meet E-2, making a fold along E-2. Blind stitch along the E-2 fold to hold it down, as in illustration 5.
8. Sew piece K inside piece J. The completed flower is shown in illustration 6.
9. Sew the completed flowers onto the background square.

M A K I N G   T H E   B U D

1. Using illustration 7 as a guide, lightly draw all lines onto piece L.
2. With the right side facing up, fold along line A, pushing the top part of the circle to the back. Fold along B-1, bringing it to meet B-2. Fold along C-1, as in illustration 8. Pin.
3. Fold along D and bring the fabric down to meet C-1 to C-2, as in illustration 9. Pin in place.
4. Lightly draw the curved line in illustration 9 onto the fabric. Fold the fabric back along this curved line. The completed bud is shown in illustration 10.
5. Sew the completed bud onto the background square.

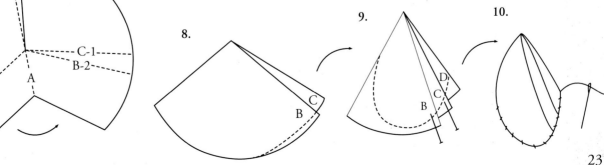

WATER LILY QUILT

QUILT SIZE:
34" x 34" *(86cm x 86cm)*

BLOCK SIZE:
14" *(36cm)*

SETTING:
2 x 2

BLOCKS:
4

FABRIC NEEDED:

Item	Yards	/Cm
Background	1	*(91)*
Template A	¼	*(23)*
Template B	¼	*(23)*
Template C	¼	*(23)*
Template D	⅛	*(11)*
Template E	⅛	*(11)*
Template F	⅛	*(11)*
Template G	¼	*(23)*
Template H	⅛	*(11)*
Template I	⅛	*(11)*
Template J	⅝	*(57)*
Template K	⅜	*(34)*
Template L	¼	*(23)*
Border 3" *(76mm)*	⅝	*(57)*

Cutting	Amount
Background and Batting	
15" x 15" *(38cm x 38cm)*	4
Template A	4
Template B	4
Template C	4
Template D	4
Template E	4
Template F	4
Template G	4
Template H	4
Template I	4
Template J	16
Template K	16
Template L	4

Border cut 3 ½" *(89mm)* including ¼" *(6mm)* seam allowance.

Use diagram as guide for assembly.

*D*EEP IN THE *forest there was a lovely meadow that no person had ever seen. For thousands of y violets had grown there. In a pond nearby lived a young alligator whose joy in life was to play played day after day, but since there was no one around to hear his music, the alligator had no idea was good or bad. So one day he visited the violets in the meadow and asked them to listen him play. H made them feel wonderful. To thank him, the violets made a wreath of blossoms for the young alligat was so pleased that silver tears rolled from his eyes.*

MAKING THE BLOCK

1. Cut a background square from templates A and B on page 109 and piece them together. This includes a ½" (13mm) seam allowance.

2. Using the rest of the templates on pages 109 and 110, lightly draw the outline of the design onto the back-

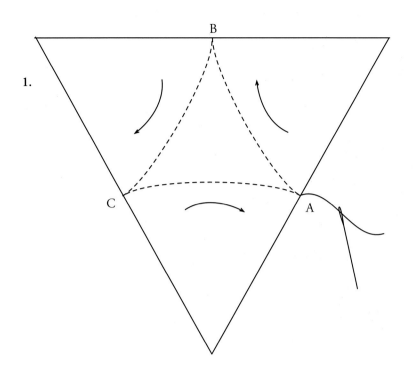

1. Sew two N pieces, right sides together, leaving an opening. Turn right side out. Blind stitch closed. Finger press seams.

2. Using template N and illustration 1, take a running stitch from A to B. Gather. Back stitch twice to hold the gathers in place.

3. In the same way, sew from B to C and from C to A. Gather each section as you go. Back stitch twice to hold the gathers in place.

4. Use a pencil or other stick-like tool to push the center of the flower down, as in illustration 2. Bring the petals up, as in illustration 3. Stuff the center of the flower with a little cotton.

5. Sew the completed flowers onto the background square.

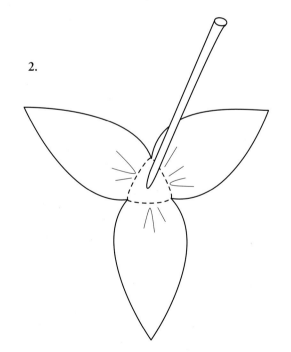

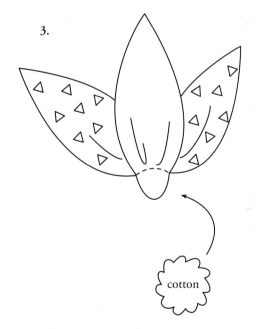

cotton

*R*ITOMU, A SMALL *black ant, had a reputation for being a hard worker. One day, exhausted from all his work, he lay down to rest. As he was resting, he looked up at the sky from the hole in the ground where he lived and dreamed of changing his life and trying something new. Refreshed and excited, he left his home behind and climbed up a dianthus flower nearby. From high up on top of the flower, he noticed that the air was cleaner and fresher than he had ever known it to be and wondered where this wonderful fresh breeze was coming from. He went home and asked his wife, Kurim, to go with him to find out. They set out on their journey, climbing higher and higher up a hill nearby, and as they reached the top they saw an enormous body of water. It was the ocean. His curiosity satisfied, Ritomu returned home with Kurim, pleased with his big adventure but glad to have a safe hole in the ground for his home.*

MAKING THE BLOCK

1. Cut two pieces of complementary fabric, 15" x 12 ½" (38cm x 32cm) and 15" x 3 ½" (38cm x 9cm), and piece them together to make the background square. This includes a ½" (13mm) seam allowance.
2. Using the templates on page 111, lightly draw the outline of the design onto the background square.
3. Copy the sashiko design from page 80 onto the background square.
4. Cut a 15" x 15" (38cm x 38cm) piece of batting. Baste it to the back of the background square.
5. Complete the sashiko as shown on the sashiko design.
6. Using the templates on page 111, cut out all pieces from selected fabrics. Add a ⅛" (3mm) seam allowance.
7. Appliqué stem A and leaves B and C.
8. Appliqué stem D, leaf E, and stem F.
9. Appliqué leaves G and H and stem I.
10. Appliqué stem J, leaves K, L, M, and N, and stem O.

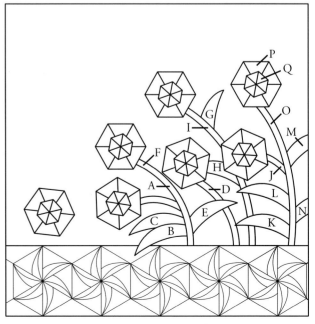

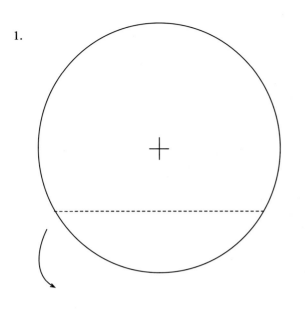

1.

1. Mark the center of piece P as shown in illustration 1.
2. Fold one edge of the circle to the center mark and pin, as shown in illustration 2.
3. Fold the next edge of the circle to the center mark and pin, as in illustration 3. Repeat four more times as shown in illustrations 4, 5, 6, and 7.
4. Tack the center to hold the edges down and sew the flower onto the background square.
5. Repeat steps 1 through 4 with piece Q. Sew this smaller piece onto the center of piece P.

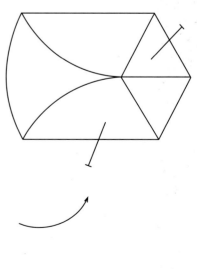

7.

6.

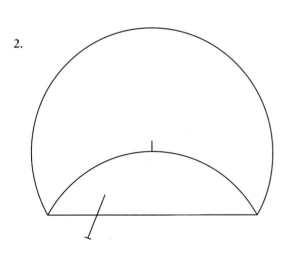

2.

5.

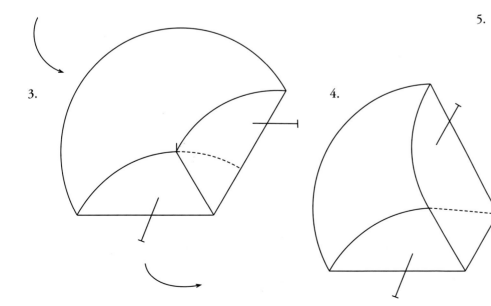

3.

4.

29

*O*N A SUMMER *afternoon, a swallowtail butterfly was flying around looking for flower nectar. She stopped on a pine branch to rest and there met an inchworm named Lerun. They chatted for a while. Lerun told the butterfly of his life-long desire to fly and she agreed to take him on her shoulders if he would show her where she could find some flowers. They flew to a clearing in the woods and there they saw thousands of Akebia flowers in full bloom. It was a wonderful day for both of them.*

MAKING THE BLOCK

1. Cut a background square 15" x 15" (38cm x 38cm). This includes a ½" (13mm) seam allowance.
2. Using the templates on page 112, lightly draw the outline of the design onto the background square.
3. Copy the sashiko design from page 81 onto the background square.
4. Cut a 15" x 15" (38cm x 38cm) piece of cotton or polyester batting. Baste it to the back of the background square.
5. Complete the sashiko as shown on the sashiko design.
6. Using the templates on page 112, cut out all pieces from selected fabrics. Add ⅛" (3mm) seam allowance.
7. Appliqué stems A, B, C, D, E, F, G, and H.
8. Appliqué leaf I and four leaves J.

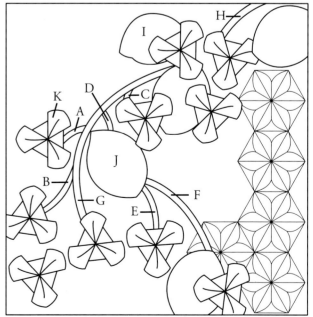

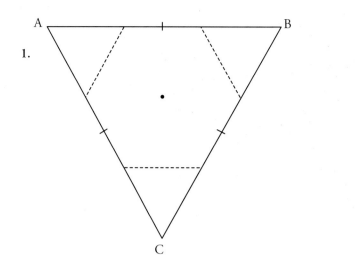

1.

1. Sew two K pieces, right sides together, one from light fabric, one from dark. Leave an opening. Turn right side out through the opening. Blind stitch closed. Finger press seams.
2. Fold each point of the triangle into the center along the dotted lines, as shown in illustrations 1 through 4.
3. Tack the points together at the center.
4. Turn the flower over. Pull point D into the center and pin to hold in place, as in illustration 5. Repeat for points E and F, as in illustrations 6 and 7.
6. Tack the points together at the center.
7. Sew the completed flowers onto the background square.

2.

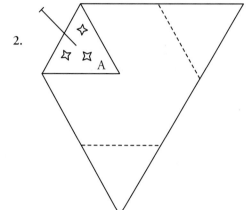

7.

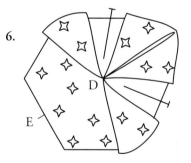

3.

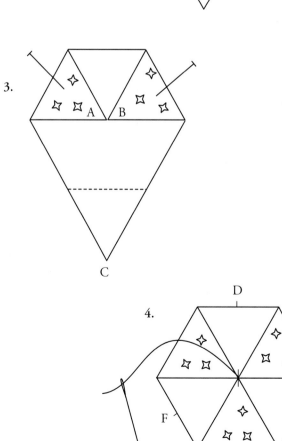

6.

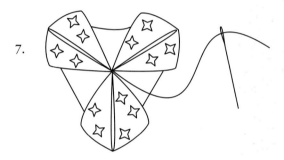

5.

4.

31

*I*N THE CENTER *of a small village deep in the mountains of Kanoko there stands an ancient star tree. Its flowers bloom only one night a year during the full moon. The flowers look like tiny lanterns, glowing in the darkness. On the night that the tree blooms, all the creatures nearby come together to celebrate. The dayflies wear their party clothes and the bees bring plenty of honey for everyone to enjoy. The crickets play sweet music all night long. When it's time to go home, the fireflies help all the creatures find their way.*

MAKING THE BLOCK

1. Cut a background square 15" x 15" (38cm x 38cm). This includes a ½" (13mm) seam allowance.
2. Using the templates on page 113, lightly draw the outline of the design onto the background square.
3. Copy the sashiko design from page 81 onto the background square.
4. Cut a 15" x 15" (38cm x 38cm) piece of cotton or polyester batting. Baste it to the back of the background square.
5. Complete the sashiko as shown on the sashiko design.
6. Using the templates on page 113, cut out all pieces from selected fabrics. Add a ⅛" (3mm) seam allowance.
7. Appliqué one leaf A, two leaves B, and three leaves C.
8. Appliqué stems D, E, F, G, H, I, and J.

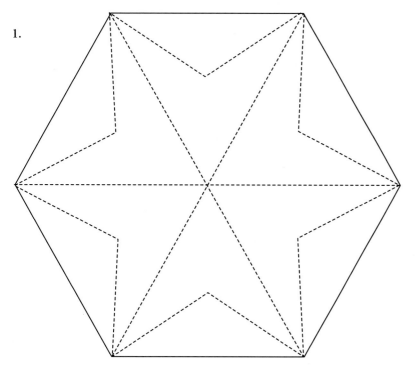

1.

1. Sew two K pieces, right sides together. Leave an opening and turn right side out through the opening. Blind stitch the opening. Finger press the seams.
2. Lightly trace a six-pointed star onto the flower, as shown in illustration 1.
3. Using a running stitch, sew from A to B, as in illustration 2. Gather, then back stitch twice to hold the gathers.
4. Repeat this procedure around the star, sewing from B to C, C to D, D to E, E to F, F to G, G to H, H to I, I to J, J to K, K to L, and L to A.
5. At each point of the star, pull adjoining fabric together and tack, as in illustration 3.
6. Sew the completed flowers onto the background square.

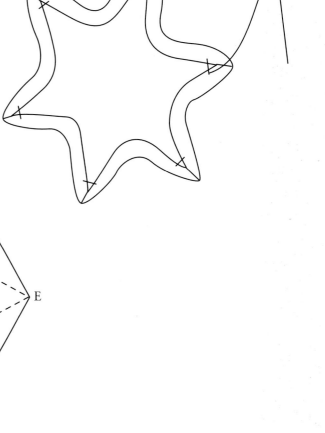

3.

2.

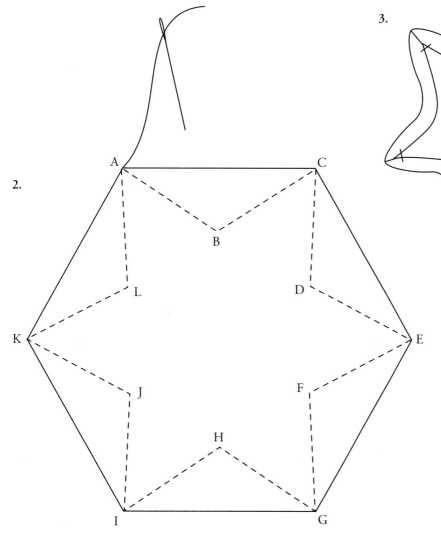

33

*T*he petals of the poppy flower are as thin as tissue paper. Before the flower blooms, all the petals are carefully wrapped together inside an egg-shaped bud. It usually takes some time for the bud to open, as the spring winds gently blow, trying to awaken it. But early one morning as the sun begins to rise, the bud begins to unfold, opening itself to the world. It soon discovers there are thousands upon thousands of poppy flowers all around, turning the green hills into a glorious array of bright colors. This scene is so spectacular it is hard to believe it is real.

MAKING THE BLOCK

1. Cut a background square 15" x 15" (38cm x 38cm). This includes a ½" (13mm) seam allowance.
2. Using the templates on pages 114 and 115, lightly draw the outline of the design onto the background square.
3. Copy the sashiko design from page 82 onto the background square.
4. Cut a 15" x 15" (38cm x 38cm) piece of cotton or polyester batting. Baste it to the back of the background square.
5. Complete the sashiko as shown on the sashiko design.
6. Using the templates on pages 114 and 115, cut out all pieces. Add a ⅛" (3mm) seam allowance.
7. Appliqué stems A, B, C, D, E, and F.
8. Appliqué leaves G and leaves H and I.
9. Sew piece K to the end of piece J. Appliqué onto the background square, stuffing each bud with a small piece of cotton to make it slightly puffy.

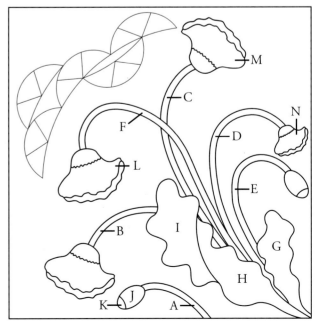

Make 4
Make one flower from template L, two from template M,
and one from template N. Use one light-colored fabric and
one dark-colored fabric for each flower.

1. Place two pieces cut from same template right sides together. Sew around them, leaving an opening. Turn right side out through the opening. Blind stitch the opening closed. Finger press the seam.
2. For templates L and M, stitch along the lines shown in illustration 1. Pull the thread to gather the fabric as shown. Fold each circle in half. Sew the flowers from templates L and M onto the background square.
3. For template N, stitch around the circle as shown in illustration 2. Pull the thread to gather the fabric. Stuff a little cotton in the center of the circle. Stitch around the circle just above the cotton. Pull the thread to gather the fabric. Attach the flower to the background square.

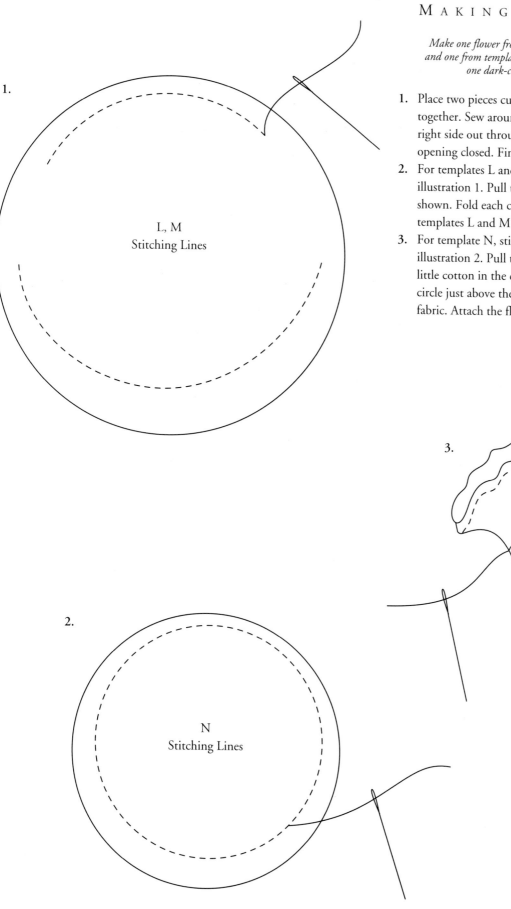

1.

L, M
Stitching Lines

2.

N
Stitching Lines

3.

A

cotton

POPPY QUILT

QUILT SIZE:
34" x 34" (86cm x 86cm)

BLOCK SIZE:
14" (36cm)

SETTING:
2 x 2

BLOCKS:
4

FABRIC NEEDED:

Item	Yards	/Cm
Background	1	(91)
Template A	⅛	(11)
Template B	⅛	(11)
Template C	⅛	(11)
Template D	⅛	(11)
Template E	¼	(23)
Template F	¼	(23)
Template G	⅛	(11)
Template H	⅛	(11)
Template I	⅛	(11)
Template J	⅛	(11)
Template K	⅛	(11)
Template L	⅜	(34)
Template M	¼	(23)
Template N	⅛	(11)
Border 3" (76mm)	⅝	(57)

Cutting	Amount
Background and Batting	
15" x 15" (38cm x 38cm)	4
Template A	4
Template B	4
Template C	4
Template D	4
Template E	4
Template F	4
Template G	4
Template H	4
Template I	4
Template J	8
Template K	8
Template L	8
Template M	16
Template N	8

Border width cut 3 ½" (89mm) including ¼" (6mm) seam allowance.

Use diagram as guide for assembly.

*O*NE SUMMER THE *blossoms on the bottle gourd were more beautiful than they had ever been befor*
exquisite. The blossoms were excited to see who would come to visit them and admire them. Firs
geous humming bird to taste their sweet nectar. Next come a flock of small birds to sit and rest for a
shade of the beautiful blossoms. Of course, busy bees flew by every day. One day a big bumble bee
buried his nose in each of the flowers. When he had finished his face was full of yellow pollen. When
his wife and children all laughed at their father's yellow face.

M A K I N G   T H E   B L O C K

1. Cut a background square 15" x 15" (38cm x 38cm). This includes a ½" (13mm) seam allowance.

2. Using the templates on page 116, lightly draw the out-

1. Sew two G pieces, right sides together. Leave an opening and turn right side out through the opening. Blind stitch the opening. Finger press the seams.

2. Divide circle G into six equal pieces and lightly draw the lines shown in illustration 1. Mark 1" (25mm) from the outside of the circle on each line.

3. Fold the circle along one of the lines, right sides together. Stitch ⅛" (3mm) from the fold line, from the edge of the circle to the 1" (25mm) mark at the end of the fold, as shown in illustration 2.

4. Fold the circle along the next line, right sides together, and stitch again as in step 2.

5. Repeat around the circle until you have stitched six 1" (25mm) lines. Finger press the folds to one side. Turn right side up. The completed flower is shown in illustration 3.

6. Sew the flowers onto the background square at the ends of the calyxes.

1.

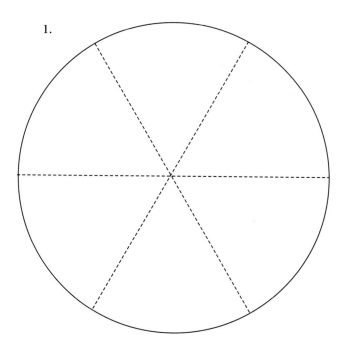

2.

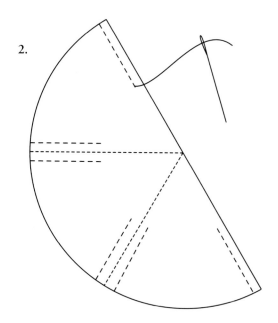

3.

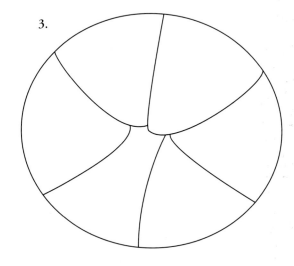

*M*R. BUMBLEBEE LIKED *to brag to his friends about all the different flowers he knew by name. He was proud of the fact that he had visited them all. One day a dragonfly told Mr. Bumblebee about a flower he had never heard of nor seen. This particular flower, the flaming lily, grew only among the rocks high in the mountains, where a fierce wind blows. Mr. Bumblebee had to see this special flower and so he set off for the mountains to find it. He searched and searched and at last he found the plant. The buds were closed so Mr. Bumblebee settled down to wait for them to bloom. When the blossoms opened, he was amazed to see how beautiful the flaming lily was. He decided never again to brag about the number of different flowers he knew. He had realized to his joy that there will always be another wonderful flower somewhere in the world, waiting to be discovered.*

MAKING THE BLOCK

1. Cut a background square 15" x 15" (38cm x 38cm). This includes a ½" (13mm) seam allowance.
2. Using the templates on page 117, lightly draw the outline of the design onto the background square.
3. Copy the sashiko design from page 83 onto the background square.
4. Cut a 15" x 15" (38cm x 38cm) piece of cotton or polyester batting. Baste it to the back of the background square.
5. Complete the sashiko as shown on the sashiko design.
6. Using the templates on page 117, cut out all pieces from selected fabrics. Add a ⅛" (3mm) seam allowance.
7. Appliqué stems A and B.
8. Appliqué bud C and the bud made up from pieces D and E.
9. Appliqué five leaves F and one leaf G.
10. Appliqué stem H.

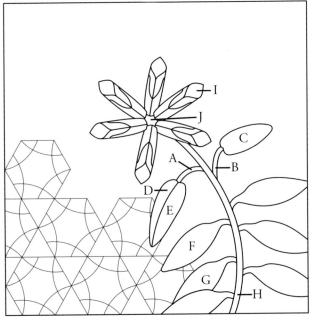

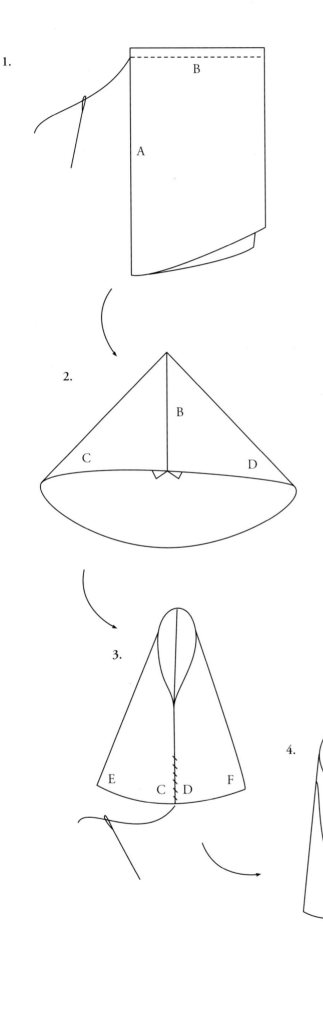

MAKING THE FLOWER
Make six petals, following steps 1 to 7.

1. Fold piece I in half, right sides together.
2. Sew along the top edge B, as shown in illustration 1.
3. Turn right side out, with line B in the center, as in illustration 2. Finger press the fold lines from the top of B to C and D.
4. Bring corners C and D to the center. Sew from the bottom of the piece up 1" (25mm) towards the point, as shown in illustration 3.
5. Bring corners E and F to the center. Sew from the bottom of the piece up ½" (13mm) towards the point, as shown in illustration 4.
6. Using a running stitch, sew across the bottom of the petal, as in illustration 5.
7. Gather the petal bottom to close it, as in illustration 6.
8. Using a running stitch, sew along the dotted line on piece J as in illustration 7. Pull the thread to gather. Sew this piece onto the background square at the flower's center. Attach the six petals.

41

*L*ERUN THE INCHWORM *was taking an afternoon nap on the branch of a bindweed plant that grew in the back yard of the baker's house. In his dream, a little girl, the baker's daughter, was blowing soap bubbles. As one of the bubbles floated by, Lerun jumped on for the ride. High into the sky went the beautiful bubble, and from there Lerun could see for miles and miles across the open valley. The flowers waved to him as he sailed above them. Finally, the soap bubble and Lerun landed back where they had begun, in the baker's back yard. From then on, whenever he saw the little girl blow bubbles, Lerun imagined he was flying far, far above the bindweed tree.*

MAKING THE BLOCK

1. Cut two pieces of complementary fabric, 5 ½" x 15" (38cm x 14cm) and 10 ½" x 15" (38cm x 27cm). Piece them together to make the background square. This includes a ½" (13mm) seam allowance.
2. Using the templates on page 118, lightly draw the outline of the design onto the background square.
3. Copy the sashiko design from page 83 onto the background square.
4. Cut a 15" x 15" (38cm x 38cm) piece of batting. Baste it to the back of the background square.
5. Complete the sashiko as shown on the sashiko design.
6. Using the templates on page 118, cut out all pieces from selected fabrics. Add a ⅛" (3mm) seam allowance
7. Appliqué the leaf made up from pieces A and B, just where the two fabrics are joined.
8. Appliqué stems C, D, and E.
9. Appliqué four leaves F and two leaves G.

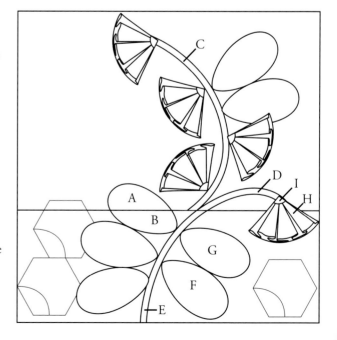

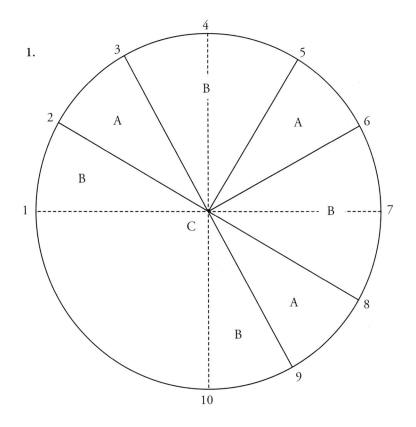

1.

1. Sew two H pieces, right sides together. Leave an opening and turn right side out through the opening. Blind stitch the opening. Finger press the seam.

2. On flower piece H, lightly draw the lines shown in illustration 1.

3. Bring point 2 to meet point 1, making a tuck in the B section. Pin to hold.

4. Bring point 3 to meet point 4, making a tuck in another B section. Pin.

5. In the same way, bring point 5 to meet point 4, point 6 to point 7, point 8 to point 7, and point 9 to point 10, pinning as you go. The flower is shown in illustration 3, with three A sections on top.

6. Sew together each A section from point C ½" (13mm) up toward the open edge.

7. Appliqué calyx I over point C, as shown in illustration 4.

8. Sew the completed flowers onto the background square.

2.

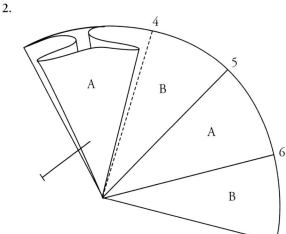

4.

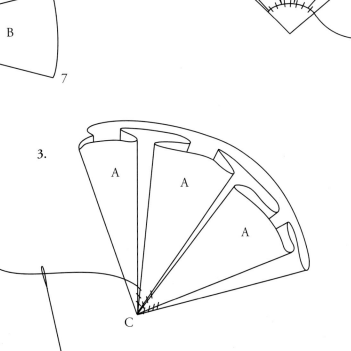

3.

43

*D*EEP IN AN *old oak forest in Ireland, there was a beautiful castle surrounded by all kinds of flowers. Most of the flowers lived a lonely life, but one fall evening they got together for an all-night party. On this special night, all the flowers celebrated by sending their seeds flying into the air, where they were carried off by the wind to the farthest corners of Ireland. As time passed, the seeds turned into sturdy plants and in the spring, when all new flowers begin to bloom, they grew together in bunches. From that time on, they laughed and danced together and called themselves Allium flowers.*

MAKING THE BLOCK

1. Cut a background square 15" x 15" (38cm x 38cm). This includes a ½" (13mm) seam allowance.
2. Using the templates on page 119, lightly draw the outline of the design onto the background square.
3. Copy the sashiko design from page 84 onto the background square.
4. Cut a 15" x 15" (38cm x 38cm) piece of cotton or polyester batting. Baste it to the back of the background square.
5. Using the templates on page 119, cut out all pieces from selected fabrics. Add a ⅛" (3mm) seam allowance.
6. Complete the sashiko as shown on the sashiko design.
7. Appliqué pieces A and B and stems C and D.
8. Make two leaves from E. Sew two E pieces for each leaf, right sides together, leaving an opening. Turn right side out. Blind stitch closed. Finger press the seams. Fold and press along the dotted line. Sew onto the background square.
9. Make five leaves from F by following above instructions. Sew onto the background square.

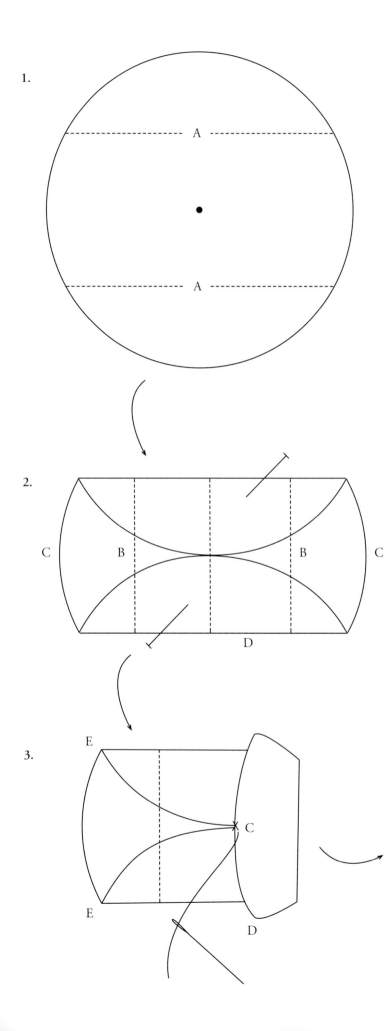

1.

2.

C   B   B   C

D

3.

E

E   C

D

Make seventeen petals, nine for the large flower using template A and eight for the small flower using template B. Follow steps 1 to 7.

1. Sew two pieces of fabric, right sides together, leaving an opening. Turn right side out through the opening. Blind stitch closed. Finger press the seam.
2. Lightly crease along dotted line A to the center of the circle, as shown in illustration 1.
3. Bring the top and bottom edges to the center of the circle, folding along dotted lines B, as in illustration 2.
4. Bring point C to the center and tack, as in illustration 3.
5. Fold points D back and spread the folds to make the petals, as in illustration 4.
6. Repeat steps 4 and 5 for the other side of the petal, points E. The completed petal is shown in illustration 5.
7. Attach the petals to the background square to create the flowers, overlapping and turning them slightly to fit.

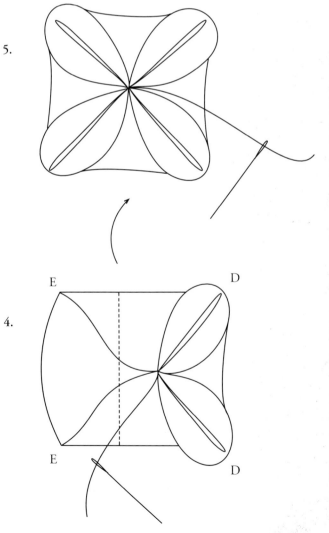

5.

4.

E   D

E   D

45

*O*NCE THERE WAS *a pond with a small fountain at its center, where two dark, lime-green tree frogs liked to play. They liked this spot so much because of the special flowers that surrounded the fountain. Their pretty blossoms hung upside down, like little straw hats, almost touching the water. The frogs played among the fountain plants and enjoyed their sweet nectar. They often had such a good time they forgot to go home.*

MAKING THE BLOCK

1. Cut a background square 17" x 17" (43cm x 43cm). This includes a ½" (13mm) seam allowance.
2. Using the templates on page 120, lightly draw the outline of the design onto the background square.
3. Copy the sashiko design from page 84 onto the background square.
4. Cut a 17" x 17" (43cm x 43cm) piece of cotton or polyester batting. Baste it to the back of the background square.
5. Complete the sashiko as shown on the sashiko design.
6. Using the templates on page 120, cut out all pieces from selected fabrics. Add a ⅛" (3mm) seam allowance.
7. Appliqué stems A, B, C, D, and E.
8. Appliqué calyxes F.
9. Appliqué leaves G.

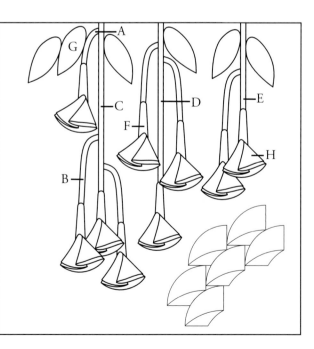

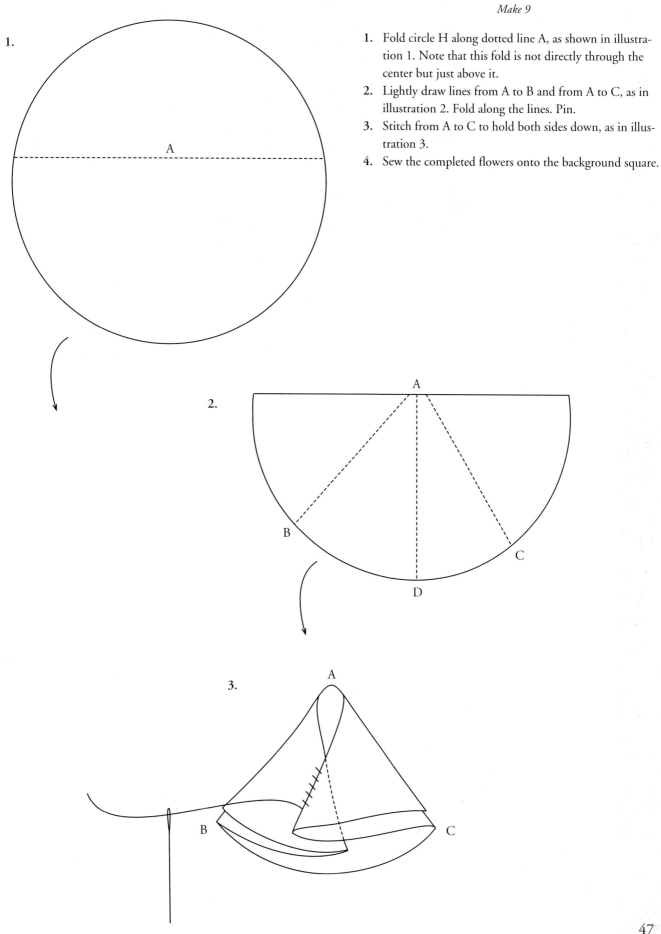

1.

1. Fold circle H along dotted line A, as shown in illustration 1. Note that this fold is not directly through the center but just above it.

2. Lightly draw lines from A to B and from A to C, as in illustration 2. Fold along the lines. Pin.

3. Stitch from A to C to hold both sides down, as in illustration 3.

4. Sew the completed flowers onto the background square.

2.

3.

FOUNTAIN PLANT QUILT

QUILT SIZE:
40" x 40" *(102cm x 102cm)*

BLOCK SIZE:
16" *(41cm)*

SETTING:
2 x 2

BLOCKS:
4

FABRIC NEEDED:

Item	Yards/Cm	
Background	1⅛	*(103)*
Batting	1⅛	*(103)*
Template A	⅛	*(11)*
Template B	¼	*(23)*
Template C	⅛	*(11)*
Template D	⅛	*(11)*
Template E	⅛	*(11)*
Template F	¼	*(23)*
Template G	¼	*(23)*
Template H	½	*(46)*
Border 4" *(102mm)*	¾	*(69)*

Cutting	Amount
Background and Batting	
17" x 17" *(43cm x 43cm)*	4
Template A	4
Template B	16
Template C	4
Template D	4
Template E	4
Template F	36
Template G	24
Template H	36

Border width cut 4 ½" *(114 mm)* including ¼" *(6mm)* seam allowance.

Use diagram as guide for assembly.

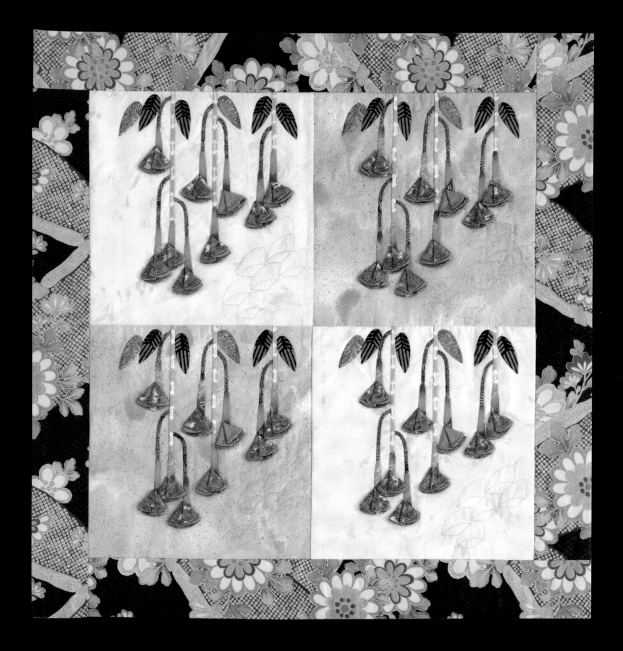

*T*HERE WAS AN *old woman who had worked hard all her life. She had a beautiful vegetable garden surrounded by lilies of the valley that were rather magical. Because she was old, she couldn't hear ordinary conversations very well, especially when her husband asked her to go with him to work in the fields. But she could always hear the little flowers. They would tell her the time by chiming the hours like tiny crystal bells. The old lady was the only one who could hear them, and this made her happy. No matter how hard she worked in her garden she was never lonely because of these special flowers.*

MAKING THE BLOCK

1. Cut a background square 17" x 17" (43cm x 43cm). This includes a ½" (13mm) seam allowance.
2. Using the templates on pages 120 to 122, lightly draw the outline of the design onto the background square.
3. Copy the sashiko design from page 85 onto the background square.
4. Cut a 17" x 17" (43cm x 43cm) piece of cotton or polyester batting. Baste it to the back of the background square.
5. Complete the sashiko as shown on the sashiko design.
6. Using the templates on pages 120 to 122, cut out all pieces from selected fabrics. Add a ⅛" (3mm) seam allowance.
7. Appliqué leaves A, B, C, D, E, and F.
8. Appliqué stems G and H and leaves I and J.
9. Appliqué stem K and leaves L and M.

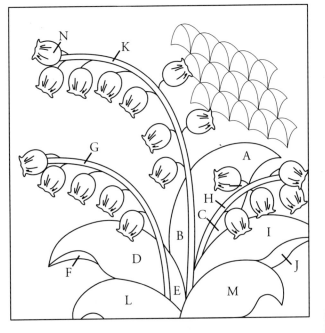

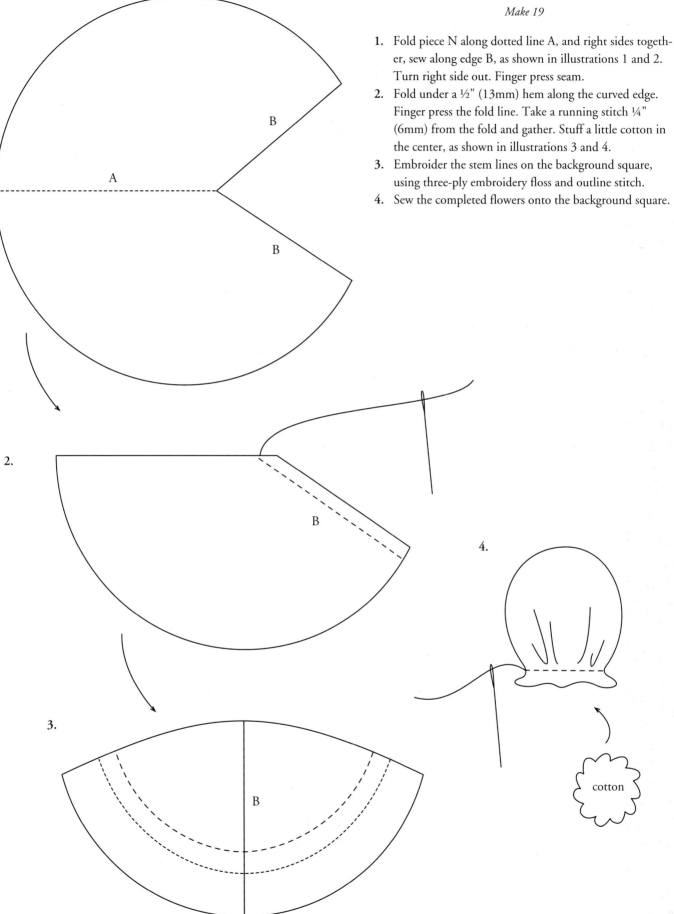

1. Fold piece N along dotted line A, and right sides together, sew along edge B, as shown in illustrations 1 and 2. Turn right side out. Finger press seam.

2. Fold under a ½" (13mm) hem along the curved edge. Finger press the fold line. Take a running stitch ¼" (6mm) from the fold and gather. Stuff a little cotton in the center, as shown in illustrations 3 and 4.

3. Embroider the stem lines on the background square, using three-ply embroidery floss and outline stitch.

4. Sew the completed flowers onto the background square.

1.

2.

3.

4.

cotton

51

A LONG TIME AGO, *a fly thought he would take a nap on a thistle flower. He loved the softness and the beautiful purple color of the flower. But as he was landing on the flower, the fly accidentally struck his bottom on one of the plant's sharp needles. Hurt and upset, he waited for the wound to heal. To his great surprise and delight, he discovered that his bottom now glowed in the dark. In gratitude to the thistle for this special gift, he decided to become a night guide for all small creatures. To this day, we can see his descendants, which we now call fireflies, working hard throughout the night.*

M A K I N G   T H E   B L O C K

1. Cut a background square 15" x 15" (38cm x 38cm). This includes a ½" (13mm) seam allowance.
2. Using the templates on page 123, lightly draw the outline of the design onto the background square.
3. Copy the sashiko design from page 85 onto the background square.
4. Cut a 15" x 15" (38cm x 38cm) piece of cotton or polyester batting. Baste it to the back of the background square.
5. Complete the sashiko as shown on the sashiko design.
6. Using the templates on page 123, cut out all pieces from selected fabrics. Add a ⅛" (3mm) seam allowance.
7. Appliqué stems A, B, and C.
8. Appliqué leaves D, E, and F and stem G.
9. Appliqué leaf H and two leaves I.

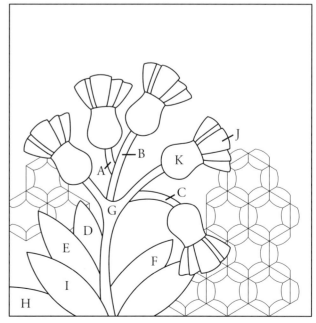

1. Sew two J pieces, right sides together. Leave an opening and turn right side out through the opening. Blind stitch the opening. Finger press the seams.
2. Mark pleats A, B, and C on piece J, as shown in illustration 1.
3. Stitch the pleats as shown in illustration 2. Stitch as far as the marks to hold the pleats in place.
4. Sew piece J onto the background square.
5. Sew piece K onto the background square over the bottom of piece J, as in illustration 3. Stuff with a little piece of cotton before the final stitches are made.

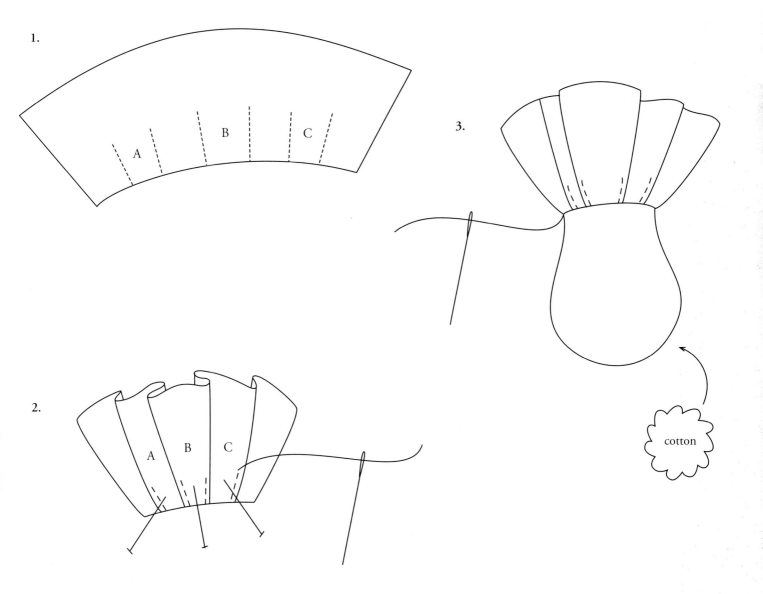

1.

2.

3.

cotton

A BEAUTIFUL CLEMATIS PLANT *grew up the side of a large white house. The three blossoms growing on it were sisters. When they were not competing with each other to decide which one of them was the most beautiful, they worried about their brother, the vine. Their brother loved to climb and would climb up anything he could reach. Might he not go too far on his climbing expeditions? Would the owner of the house cut him down for being too tall? As it turned out, to everyone's delight, the owner loved clematis flowers and wanted the plant to grow as high as it possibly could.*

MAKING THE BLOCK

1. Cut two pieces of complementary fabric, 13 ½" x 17" (43cm x 34cm) and 4 ½" x 17" (43cm x 11cm), and piece them together to make the background square. This includes a ½" (13mm) seam allowance.
2. Using the templates on page 124, lightly draw the outline of the design onto the background square.
3. Copy the sashiko design from page 86 onto the background square.
4. Cut a 18" x 17" (43cm x 43cm) piece of cotton or polyester batting. Baste it to the back of the background square.
5. Complete the sashiko as shown on the sashiko design.
6. Using the templates on page 124, cut out all pieces from selected fabrics. Add a ⅛" (3mm) seam allowance.
7. Embroider the stem lines onto the background square, using three-ply embroidery thread and outline stitch.
8. Bring leaves C and D together as shown in the diagram and stitch. Appliqué onto the background square.

1.

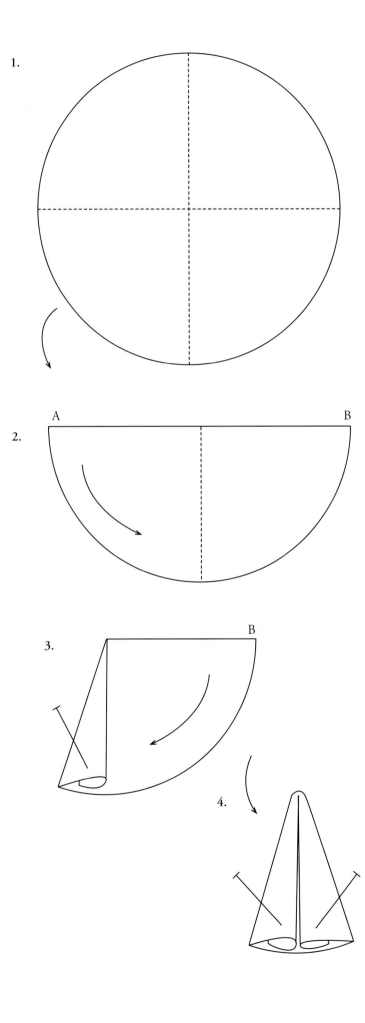

2.

A   B

3.

B

4.

Make 7

All the flower petals and buds are made the same way, using ten pieces cut from template A and fourteen pieces from template B. Use a combination of large and small petals for each full flower, arranging them in a pleasing manner as you think best.

1. Fold the circle in half. Finger press the fold. Fold the circle in half again and make a slight fold line to mark the center of the half circle. See illustrations 1 and 2.

2. Starting at point A, loosely roll the fabric to the center, as shown in illustration 3. Pin to hold. Repeat on the other side, starting at point B, as in illustration 4.

3. Stitch across the bottom of the piece, as in illustration 5. Pull the thread to gather the fabric. Back stitch twice to hold the gathers, as in illustration 6.

4. Sew three flower buds cut from template A onto the background square. Appliqué a piece F onto the end of each one, stuffing a little cotton inside to make it puffy.

5. Sew three petals cut from template B onto the background square to make the budding flower in the upper right-hand corner. Appliqué piece G to the bottom of the petals, stuffing a little cotton inside.

6. Sew six petals for each full flower onto the background square. Appliqué a piece E in the center of each, stuffing a little cotton inside.

6.

5.

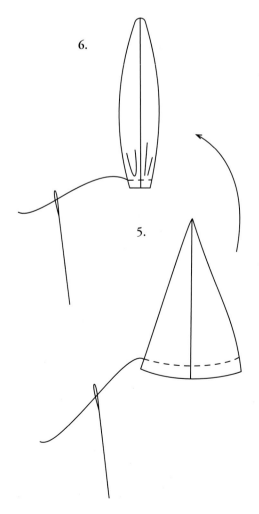

*O*NCE THERE WAS *a little kitten so happy just to be alive that she simply could not sit still. All day long she jumped, ran, and chased her tail, sometimes watching herself in the large mirror in Grandmother's bedroom. Outside the window grew a flower with no name. The flower watched the little kitten and thought how much fun it would be to act just like that. One day when the wind blew, the flower began to jump and dance. Grandmother looked out the window and saw the plant acting just like her playful kitten. She named the flower the red-hat cat-tail.*

MAKING THE BLOCK

1. Cut a background square 17" x 17" (43cm x 43cm). This includes a ½" (13mm) seam allowance.
2. Using the templates on pages 125 and 126, lightly draw the outline of the design onto the background square.
3. Copy the sashiko design from page 86 onto the background square.
4. Cut a 17" x 17" (43cm x 43cm) piece of cotton or polyester batting. Baste it to the back of the background square.
5. Complete the sashiko as shown on the sashiko design.
6. Using the templates on pages 125 and 126, cut out all pieces from selected fabrics. Add a ⅛" (3mm) seam allowance.
7. Appliqué leaves A and B.
8. Appliqué stems C, D, E, and F.
9. Appliqué leaves G, H, I, J, K, L, and M.

Make 11
Use template N to make eight large flowers and
template O to make three smaller flowers.

1. Sew one piece P to the top of each N and O piece. Finger press the seam.
2. Fold each piece in half lengthwise, right sides together. Sew the long edge, as shown in illustration 1. Turn right side out. Finger press the seam.
3. Stitch across the top of the flower, as shown in illustration 2. Pull the thread to gather, as in illustration 3.
4. Fold the bottom of the flower to the inside along the dotted line to make a hem. Finger press the fold.
5. Sew the completed flowers onto the background square.

1.   2.   3.

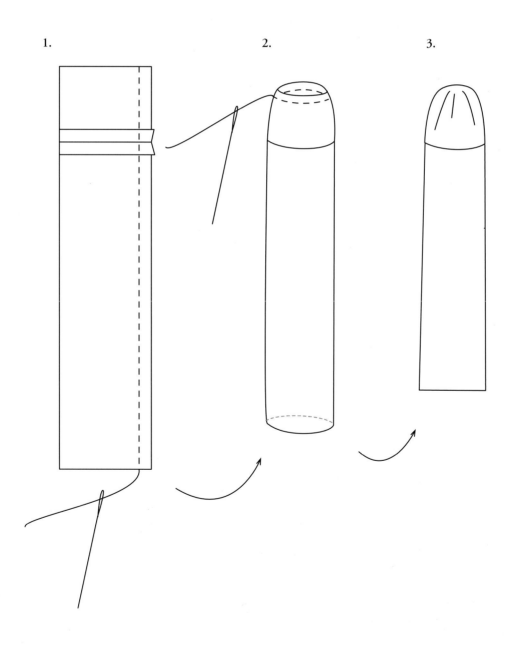

*A*N OLD MAN *lived by himself in a small cottage near a village. Every year, white hydrangeas bloomed in his garden and he never failed to water them, for he loved them very much. One year a severe drought came to the land and there was no water to give to his precious flowers. Seeing how unhappy the old man was, the birds who came to his garden brought berries in their beaks. The old man picked up the berries and squeezed them for their juice, which he then gave to his white hydrangeas. The following year, something wonderful happened: when the hydrangeas began to bloom, they were no longer white, but pink, blue, and purple instead. When the birds returned to his garden, they thought it was paradise.*

MAKING THE BLOCK

1. Cut a background square 17" x 17" (43cm x 43cm). This includes a ½" (13mm) seam allowance.
2. Using the templates on pages 127 and 128, lightly draw the outline of the design onto the background square.
3. Copy the sashiko design from page 87 onto the background square.
4. Cut a 17" x 17" (43cm x 43cm) piece of cotton or polyester batting. Baste it to the back of the background square.
5. Complete the sashiko as shown on the sashiko design.
6. Using the templates on pages 127 and 128, cut out all pieces from selected fabrics. Add a ⅛" (3mm) seam allowance.
7. Appliqué leaves A, B, D, E, and F.
8. Appliqué stem G onto leaf B.
9. Appliqué leaf C onto leaf B and stem G.

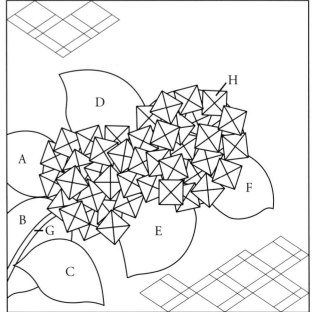

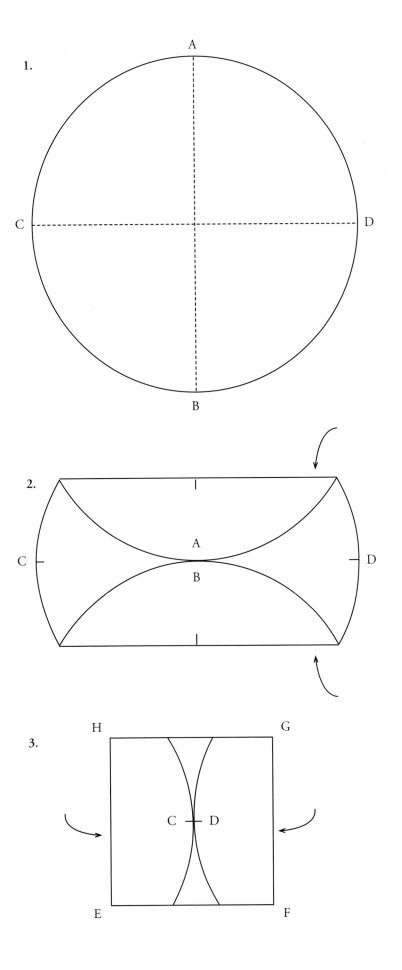

1.

2.

3.

MAKING THE FLOWERS
Make 44

1. Using piece H, bring points A and B together in the center of the circle and pin, as in illustrations 1 and 2.
2. Bring points C and D together in the center and pin, as in illustration 3.
3. Bring points E, F, G, and H together in the center and tack through all thicknesses to hold, as shown in illustrations 4 and 5.
4. Sew all flowers onto the background square.

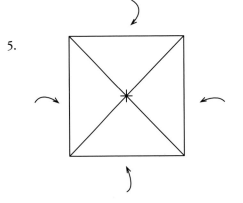

5.

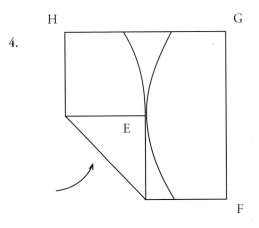

4.

HYDRANGEA QUILT

QUILT SIZE:
61 ½ " x 23 ½ " (156cm x 60cm)

BLOCK SIZE:
16 " (41cm)

SETTING:
1 x 3

BLOCKS:
3

FABRIC NEEDED:

Item	Yards/Cm	
Background	1⅛	(103)
Batting	1⅛	(103)
Template A	⅛	(11)
Template B	¼	(23)
Template C	¼	(23)
Template D	¼	(23)
Template E	¼	(23)
Template F	⅛	(11)
Template G	⅛	(11)
Template H	1½	(137)
Side border 3" (76mm)	1½	(137)
Top border 6" (152mm)	⅜	(34)
Second border ¾" (19mm)	½	(46)

Cutting	Amount
Background and Batting	
17" x 17" (43cm x 43cm)	3
Template A	3
Template B	3
Template C	3
Template D	3
Template E	3
Template F	3
Template G	3
Template H	132

Side borders cut 3 ½" (89mm) including ¼" (6mm) seam allowance.

Top borders cut 6 ½" (165mm) including ¼" (6mm) seam allowance.

Second border cut 1 ¼" (32mm) including ¼" (6mm) seam allowance.

Use diagram as guide for assembly.

A SHEPHERD BOY HAD *a special flute that he loved to play each day while caring for his sheep. One day, however, when he tried to play it, a strange sound came from the flute. He took it apart and shook it hard. Out of the flute tumbled hundreds of tiny seeds that became musical notes as they fell. When they landed on the ground, they grew into clover. From then on, whenever the shepherd boy played his flute, everyone was amazed at the wonderful music that sounded across the hills and valleys.*

MAKING THE BLOCK

1. Cut a background square 15" x 15" (38cm x 38cm). This includes a ½" (13mm) seam allowance.
2. Using the templates on pages 129 and 130, lightly draw the outline of the design onto the background square.
3. Copy the sashiko design from page 87 onto the background square.
4. Cut a 15" x 15" (38cm x 38cm) piece of cotton or polyester batting. Baste it to the back of the background square.
5. Complete the sashiko as shown on the sashiko design.
6. Using the templates on pages 129 and 130, cut out all pieces from selected fabrics. Add a ⅛" (3mm) seam allowance.
7. Appliqué stems A, B, C, D, and E.
8. Appliqué leaves F, G, H, I, J, K, and L.

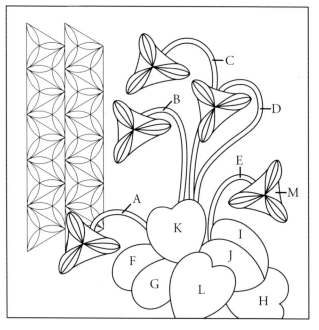

1.

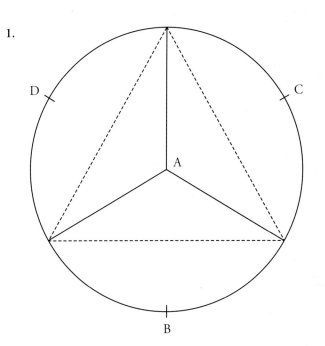

1. Sew two pieces M, right sides together, leaving an opening. Turn right side out through the opening. Blind stitch the opening closed. Finger press the seam.
2. Mark the center of the circle, A. Mark points B, C, and D, as in illustration 1.
3. Bring point B up to the center, as in illustration 2. Fold the right side flap back along dotted line E. Stitch twice in the center to hold.
4. Bring point C to the center, as in illustration 4. Fold both flaps back. Stitch twice in the center to hold.
5. Bring point D to the center. Fold flaps back. Stitch twice to hold. The complete flower is shown in illustration 5.
6. Sew the completed flowers onto the background square.

2.

5.

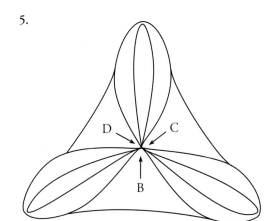

3.

4.

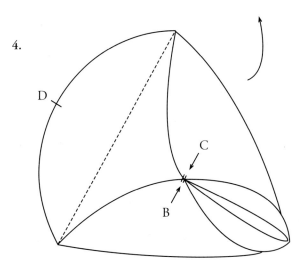

THERE ONCE WAS a plain yellow bug named Ririmu. She was shaped like a tiny half ball. Every day she flew around looking for friends to play with. Even though there were lots of honey bees in a large clover field nearby, they were always too busy collecting nectar to play. Ririmu became so lonely that she would just sit by herself at the top of the hill in the red sunset and cry. One evening, the pocketbook flowers took pity on her. As Ririmu slept that night, they dropped their red petals all around her, giving her a soft blanket to sleep on. The next morning when she awoke, Ririmu discovered she had changed into a beautiful red bug with black spots. Everyone called her Miss Ladybug and wanted to be her friend. She was never lonely again.

MAKING THE BLOCK

1. Cut a background square 17" x 17" (43cm x 43cm). This includes a ½" (13mm) seam allowance.
2. Using the templates on pages 131 and 132, lightly draw the outlines of the pattern pieces on the background square.
3. Copy the sashiko design from page 88 onto the background square.
4. Cut a 17" x 17" (43cm x 43cm) piece of cotton or polyester batting. Baste it to the back of the background square.
5. Complete the sashiko as shown on the sashiko design.
6. Using the templates on pages 131 and 132, cut out all pieces. Add a ⅛" (3mm) seam allowance.
7. Appliqué stems A, B, C, D, E, F, G, H, and I.
8. Appliqué 12 leaves J.
9. Appliqué piece K, stuffing with a little cotton. Appliqué butterfly piece L onto the background square.
10. Embroider antennae using outline stitch.

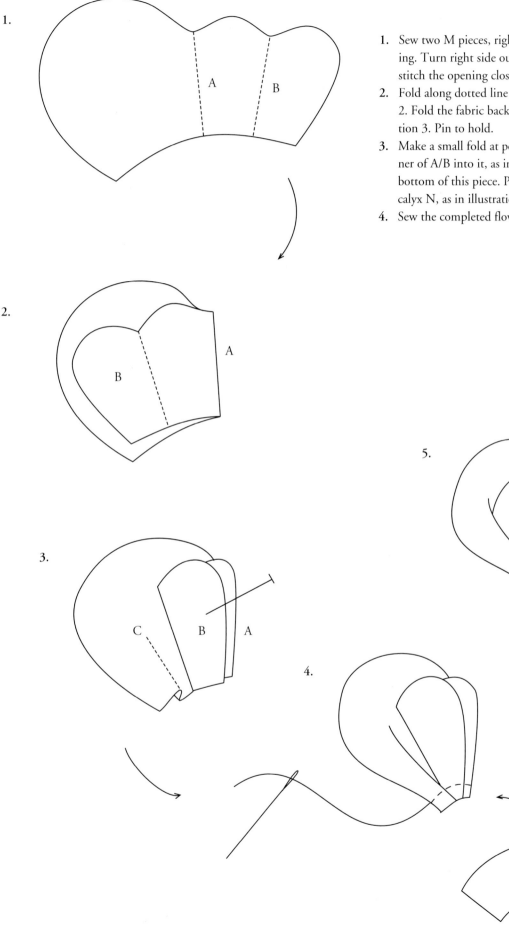

1. Sew two M pieces, right sides together, leaving an opening. Turn right side out through the opening. Blind stitch the opening closed. Finger press seams.

2. Fold along dotted line A, as shown in illustrations 1 and 2. Fold the fabric back along dotted line B, as in illustration 3. Pin to hold.

3. Make a small fold at point C and tuck the bottom corner of A/B into it, as in illustration 4. Stitch along the bottom of this piece. Pull the thread to gather. Attach calyx N, as in illustration 5.

4. Sew the completed flowers onto the background square.

*S*UMMER WAS ALMOST *over and all was quiet on the water lily pond. Karon the frog was not there. He was walking along the stream near the oak tree. A beetle family at the top of the oak called down to him, "It's a nice day, isn't it?" "Yes," Karon answered. "Better than a winter day." On either side of the stream, bush clover blooms swayed in the wind and whispered that summer was almost over. As their brightly colored leaves floated down the stream, the water bugs danced among them. The last hours of daylight faded into night.*

MAKING THE BLOCK

1. Cut a background square 17" x 17" (43cm x 43cm). This includes a ½" (13mm) seam allowance.
2. Using the templates on page 132, lightly draw the outline of the design onto the background square.
3. Copy the sashiko design from page 88 onto the background square.
4. Cut a 17" x 17" (43cm x 43cm) piece of cotton or polyester batting. Baste it to the back of the background square.
5. Complete the sashiko as shown on the sashiko design.
6. Using the templates on page 132, cut out all pieces from selected fabrics. Add a ⅛" (3mm) seam allowance.
7. Stitch the stem lines on the background square, using three-ply embroidery thread.
8. Appliqué six leaves A and eleven leaves B.

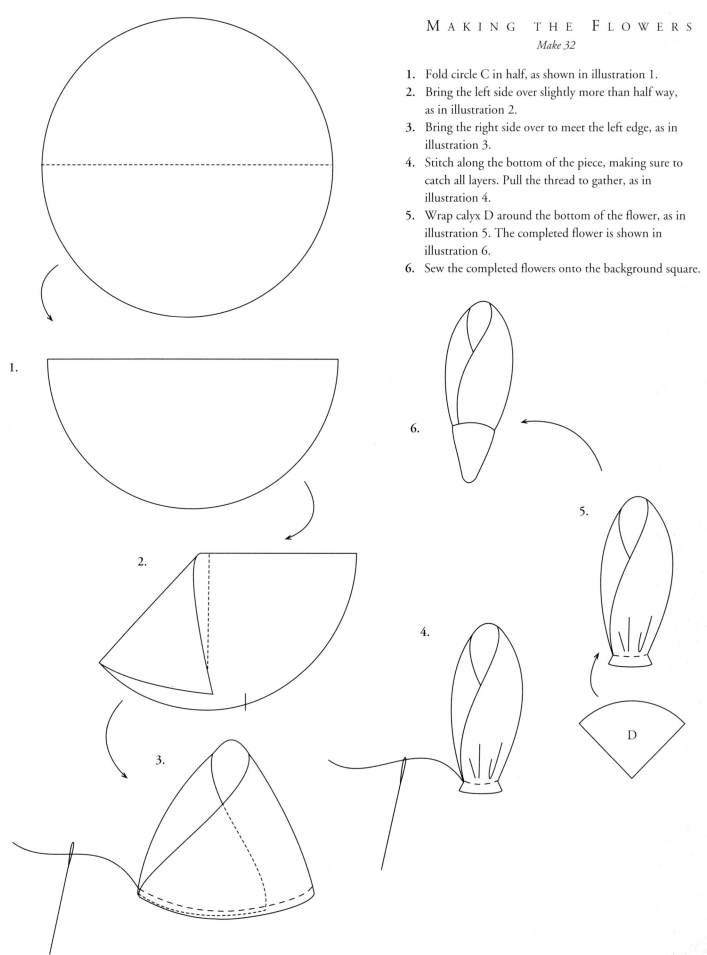

1. Fold circle C in half, as shown in illustration 1.
2. Bring the left side over slightly more than half way, as in illustration 2.
3. Bring the right side over to meet the left edge, as in illustration 3.
4. Stitch along the bottom of the piece, making sure to catch all layers. Pull the thread to gather, as in illustration 4.
5. Wrap calyx D around the bottom of the flower, as in illustration 5. The completed flower is shown in illustration 6.
6. Sew the completed flowers onto the background square.

*I*N A LARGE *green prairie surrounded by poplar trees stood a little old chapel. All around it, the Virginia bluebells rang out to announce that a wedding was to be held in the chapel. All the little creatures hurried to the church, carrying bouquets of beautiful flowers. The sky was blue, the hillside was covered with pink primroses, and everyone was happy and gay. Inside, the cricket played the organ and the firefly held his bible open. Everything was ready for the ceremony to begin. Who would the bride and groom be?*

MAKING THE BLOCK

1. Cut a background square 17" x 17" (43cm x 43cm). This includes a ½" (13mm) seam allowance.
2. Using the templates on pages 133 and 134, lightly draw the outline of the design onto the background square.
3. Copy the sashiko design from page 89 onto the background square.
4. Cut a 17" x 17" (43cm x 43cm) piece of cotton or polyester batting. Baste it to the back of the background square.
5. Complete the sashiko as shown on the sashiko design.
6. Using the templates on pages 133 and 134, cut out all pieces from selected fabrics. Add a ⅛" (3mm) seam allowance.
7. Appliqué leaves A, B, C, D, E, F, G, H, I, J, and K.
8. Appliqué stems L, M, and N.
9. Appliqué leaves O and P and stems Q and R.

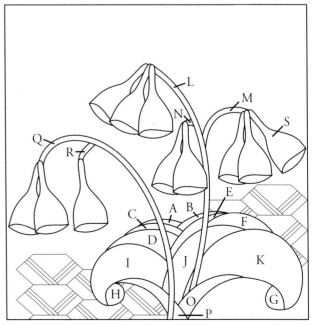

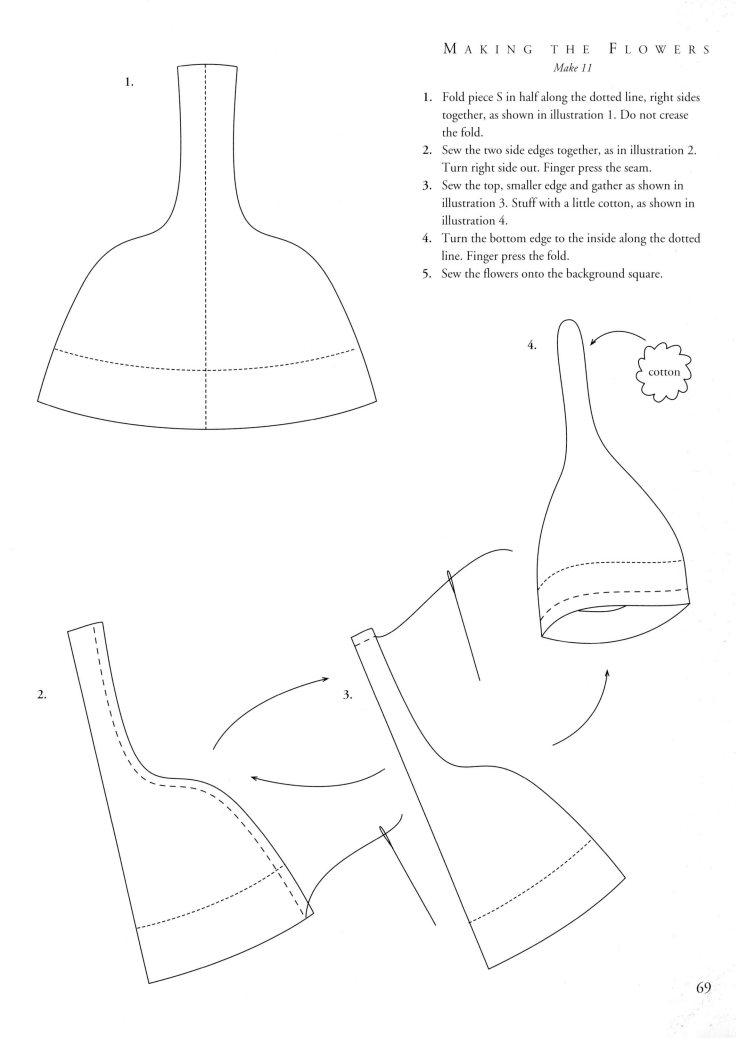

MAKING THE FLOWERS
Make 11

1. Fold piece S in half along the dotted line, right sides together, as shown in illustration 1. Do not crease the fold.
2. Sew the two side edges together, as in illustration 2. Turn right side out. Finger press the seam.
3. Sew the top, smaller edge and gather as shown in illustration 3. Stuff with a little cotton, as shown in illustration 4.
4. Turn the bottom edge to the inside along the dotted line. Finger press the fold.
5. Sew the flowers onto the background square.

cotton

1.

2.

3.

4.

*T*HE CREATURES WHO *lived in a village in the woods wanted to know which one of them was the greatest of them all. They had a festival so that they could each show off their special skills. The birds sang, the squirrels did fancy acrobatics in the trees, a cricket played his violin, and the flowers glowed with their beautiful shapes and colors. Each was good, but the village creatures could not decide which one of them was the best. They asked Queen Iris who lived beside a magical spring to help them. She threw some of the crystal water from the stream into the sky and a rainbow appeared. She said that whoever could climb or fly over it was the greatest of all. Not one of them could do it. Then Queen Iris sprinkled crystal water onto the ground and it turned into fine sand with seven colors. She said that whoever could count the grains of sand was the greatest. Of course, not one of them could do that either. The lesson they learned was that it is foolish to try to be the greatest of all. They all held hands and danced on the sand under the rainbow, happy to be who they were.*

MAKING THE BLOCK

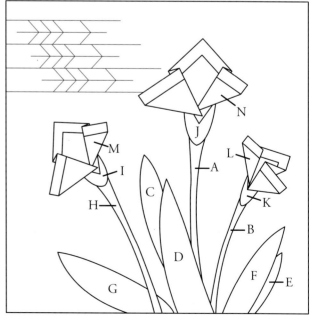

1. Cut a background square 17" x 17" (43cm x 43cm). This includes a ½" (13mm) seam allowance.
2. Using the templates on pages 135 and 136, lightly draw the outline of the design onto the background square.
3. Copy the sashiko design from page 89 onto the background square.
4. Cut a 17" x 17" (43cm x 43cm) piece of cotton or polyester batting. Baste it to the back of the background square.
5. Complete the sashiko as shown on the sashiko design.
6. Using the templates on pages 135 and 136, cut out the flower pieces from selected fabrics. Add a ⅛" (3mm) seam allowance.
7. Appliqué stems A and B.
8. Appliqué leaves C, D, E, F, and G.
9. Appliqué stem H and calyxes I, J, and K.

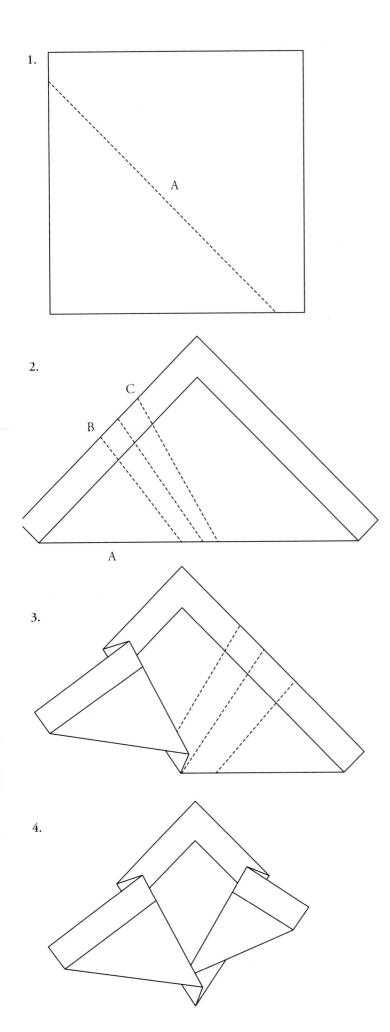

1.

2.

3.

4.

Make 3

Cut a total of six squares (three light, three dark) using templates L, M, and N. Flowers L and M are made in the same way; flower N is made slightly differently.

For each flower, sew two pattern pieces (one light, one dark) right sides together; leave an opening. Turn right side out through opening. Blind stitch the opening closed. Finger press the seams.

For flowers L and M:

1. Fold the square along dotted line A, as shown in illustration 1.
2. Make an accordion pleat on the left leg of the triangle by folding along the dotted line and bring lines B and C together, as in illustrations 2 and 3. Press.
3. Repeat on the right leg of the triangle. Tuck pleat as shown in illustration 4.

For flower N:

1. Fold the square along dotted line A.
2. Make an accordion pleat on the left leg of the triangle as shown in illustration 5. Fold along the dotted line and bring lines D and E together. Press.
3. On the right leg of the triangle, fold along the dotted line and bring F to meet dot G, as in illustration 5. Press. The completed flower is shown in illustration 6.
4. Sew the completed flowers onto the background square.

6.

5.

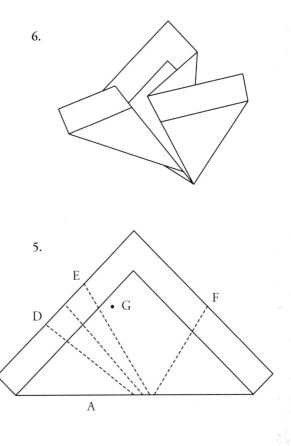

IRIS QUILT

QUILT SIZE:
30" x 56" *(76cm x 142cm)*

BLOCK SIZE:
16" *(41cm)*

SETTING:
2 x 3

BLOCKS:
3

FABRIC NEEDED:

Item	Yards/Cm	
Background	1⅛	*(103)*
Batting	1⅛	*(103)*
Template A	⅛	*(11)*
Template B	⅛	*(11)*
Template C	⅛	*(11)*
Template D	⅛	*(11)*
Template E	⅛	*(11)*
Template F	⅛	*(11)*
Template G	⅛	*(11)*
Template H	⅛	*(11)*
Template I	⅛	*(11)*
Template J	⅛	*(11)*
Template K	⅛	*(11)*
Template L	⅛	*(11)*
Template M	¼	*(23)*
Template N	¼	*(23)*
Pieced border strips to total	¼	*(23)*

Second border 4" *(102mm)* 1¾" *(160mm)*

Cutting	Amount
Background and Batting	
17" x 17" *(43cm x 43cm)*	3
Template A	3
Template B	3
Template C	3
Template D	3
Template E	3
Template F	3
Template G	3
Template H	3
Template I	3
Template J	3
Template K	3
Template L	6
Template M	6
Template N	6

Pieced border cut 2 ½" strips *(63mm)* including ¼" *(6mm)* seam allowance.

Second border cut 4 ½" *(114mm)* including ¼" *(6mm)* seam allowance.

Use diagram as guide for assembly.

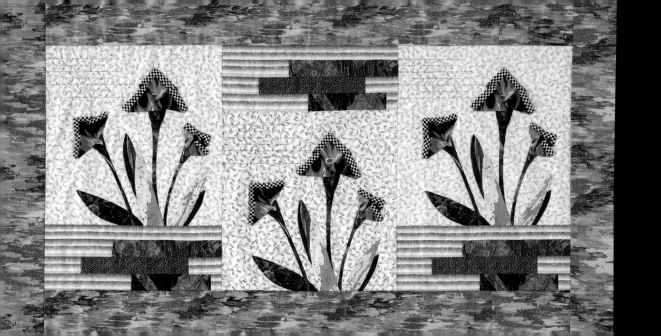

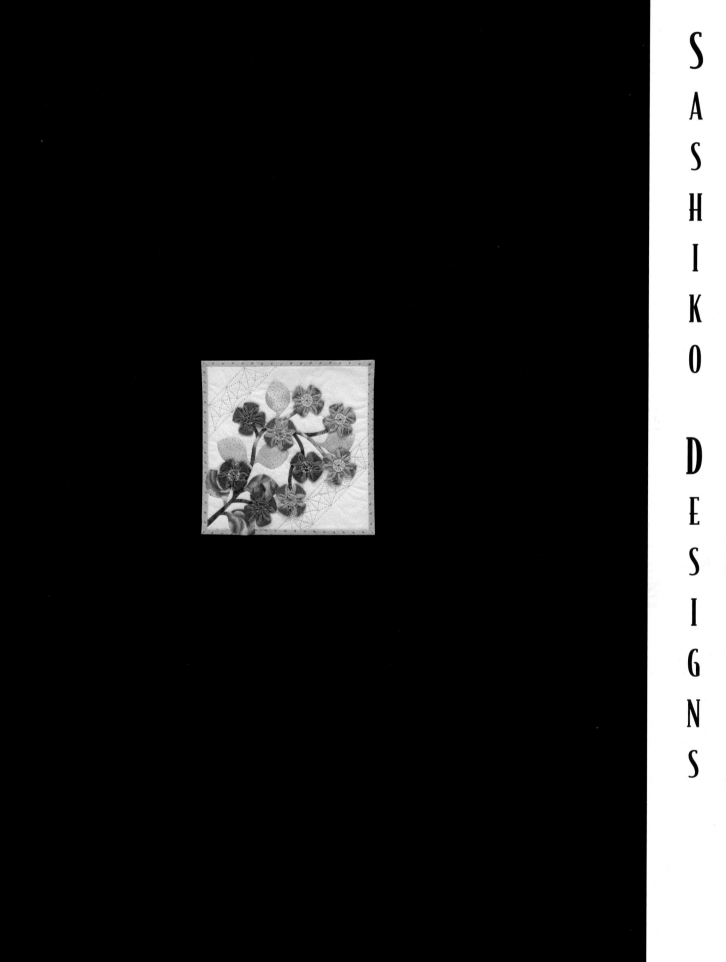

CORNFLOWER

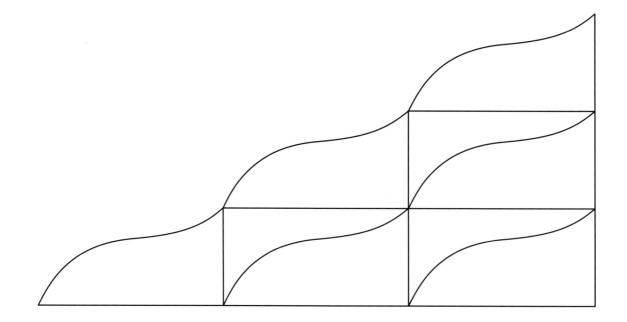

MORNING GLORY

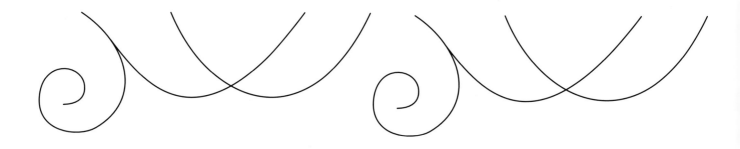

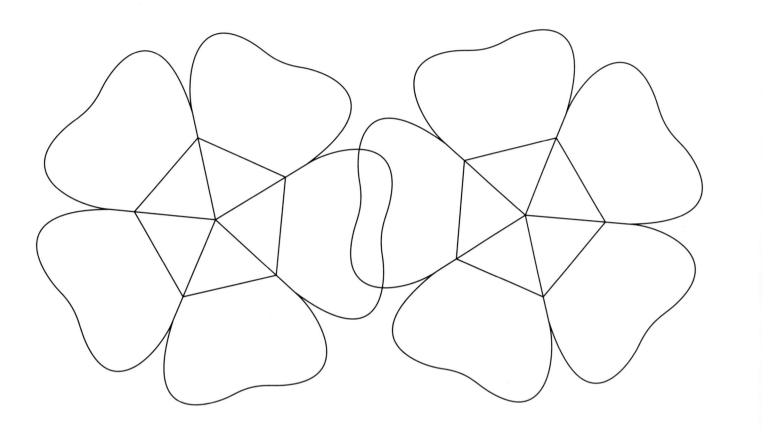

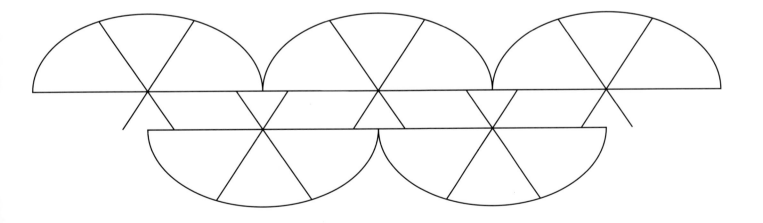

DOGWOOD

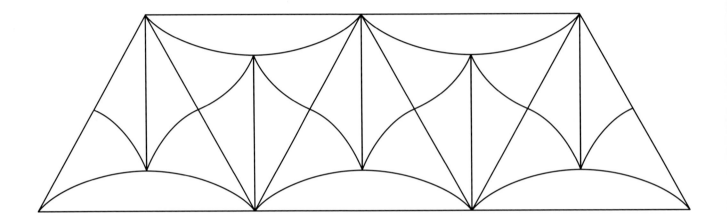

POMEGRANATE

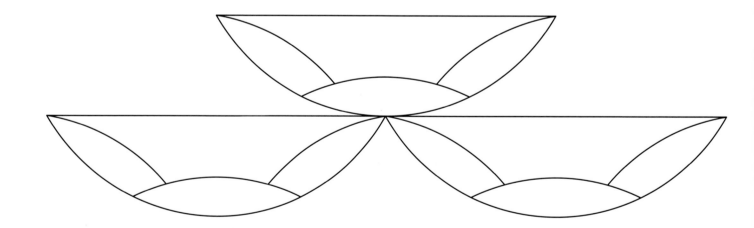

DANDELION

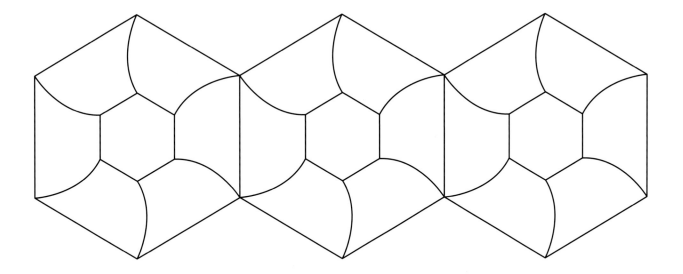

WATER LILY

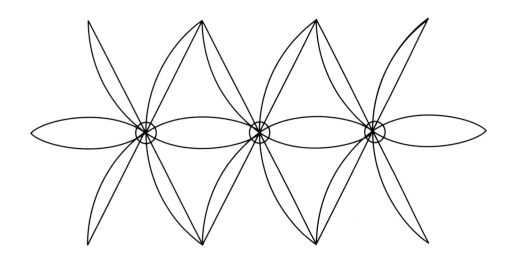

DOGTOOTH VIOLET

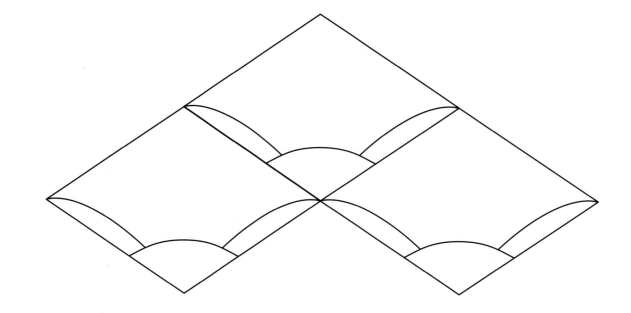

DIANTHUS

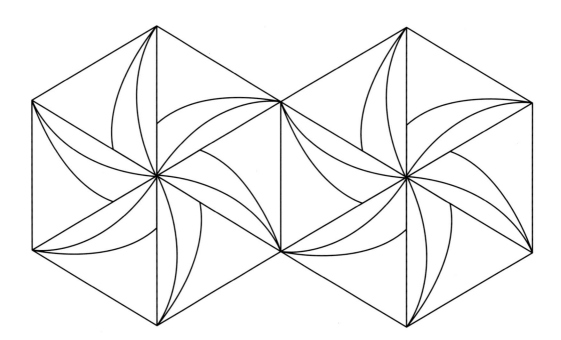

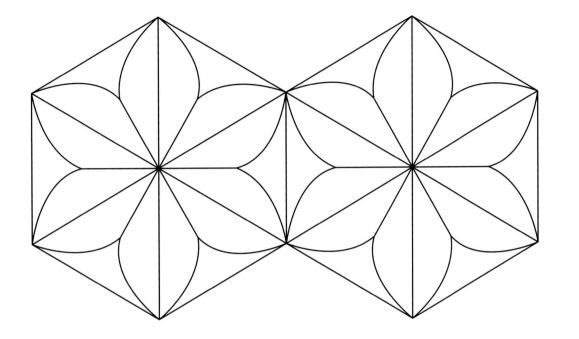

DWARF CAMPANULA

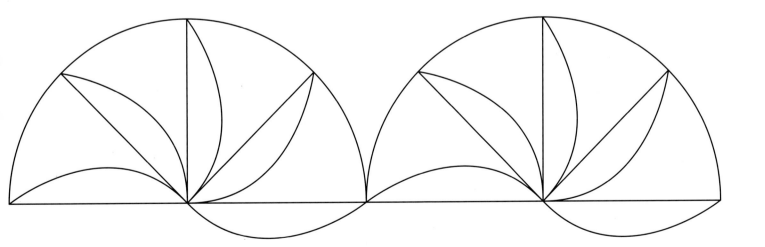

POPPY

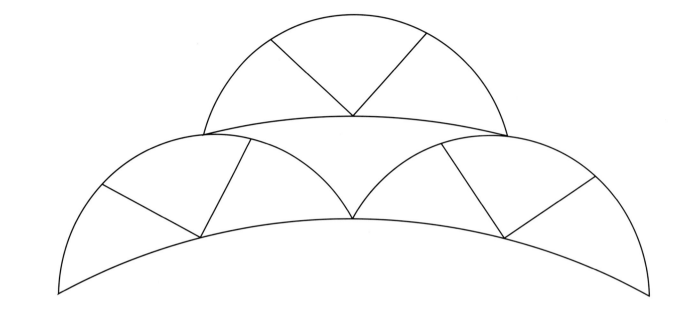

BOTTLE GOURD

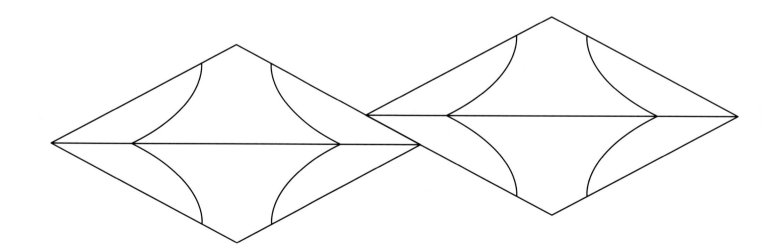

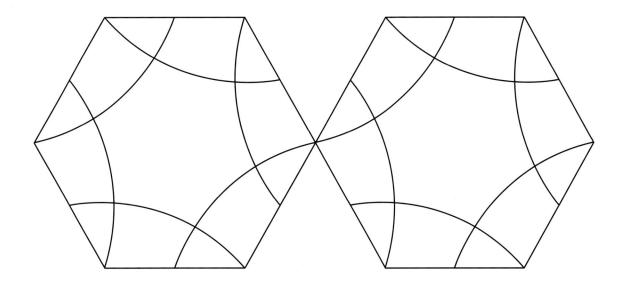

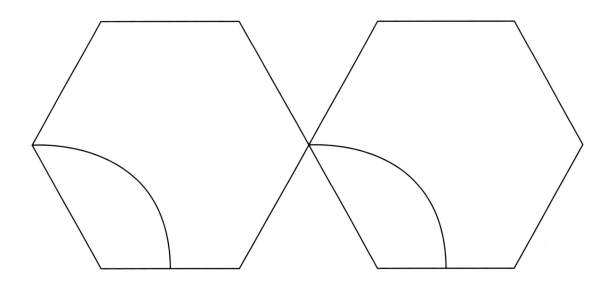

ALLIUM

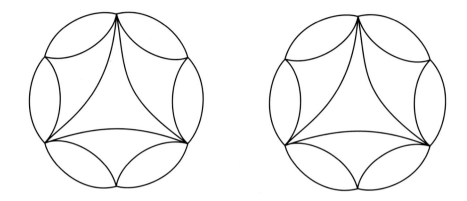

FOUNTAIN PLANT

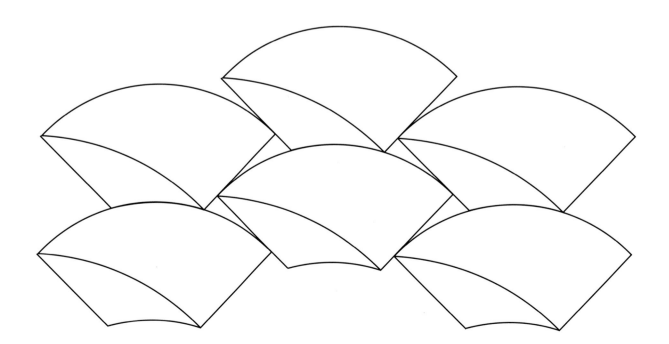

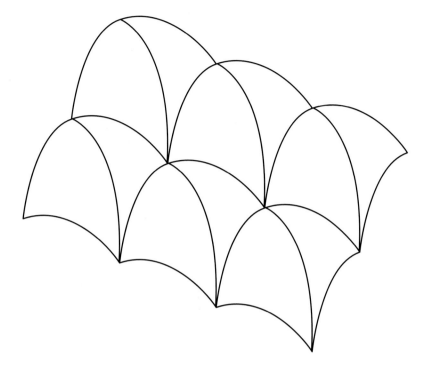

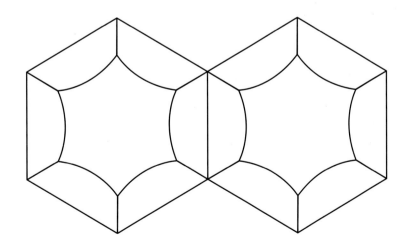

CLEMATIS

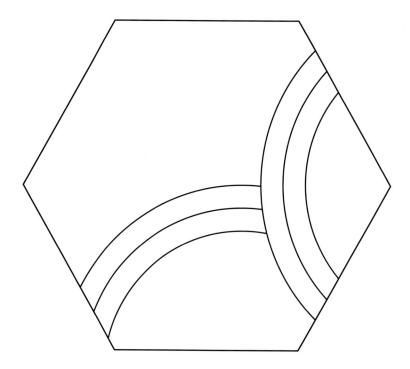

RED-HAT CAT-TAIL

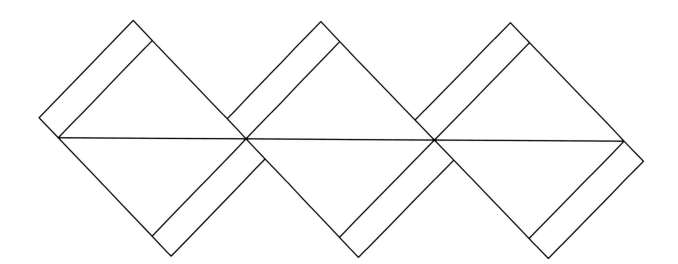

HYDRANGEA

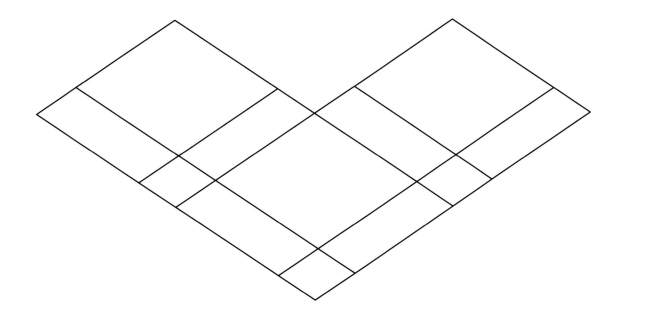

FIELD CLOVER

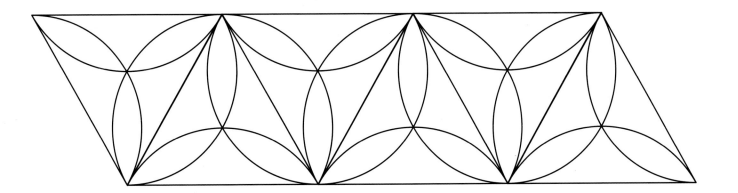

POCKETBOOK

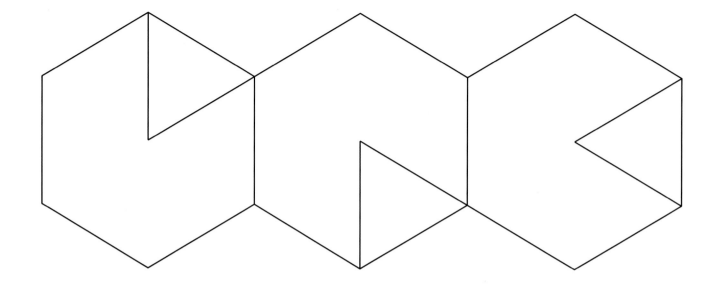

BUSH CLOVER

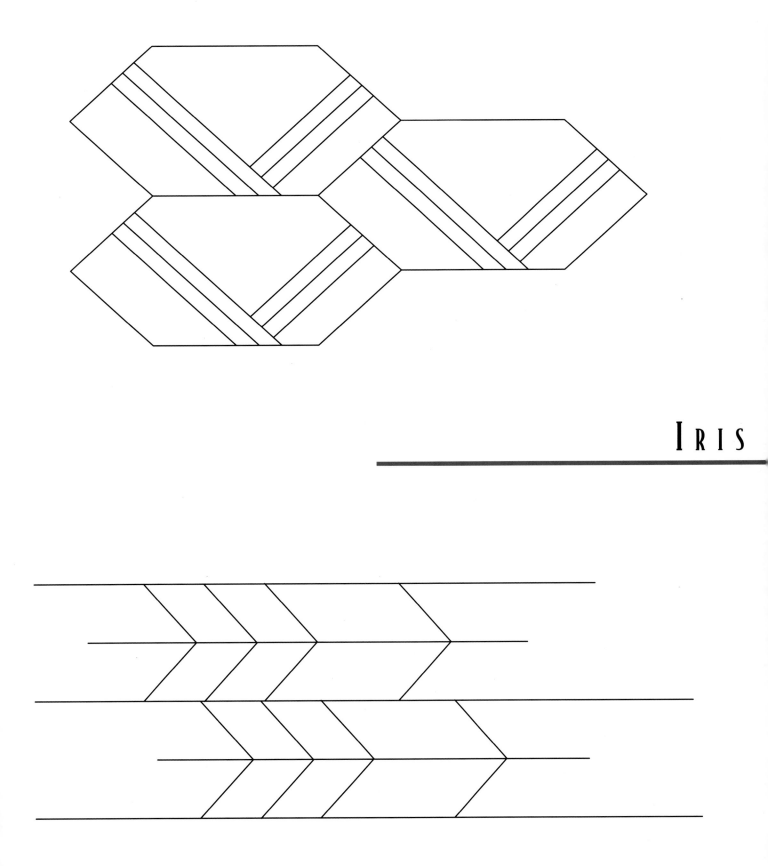

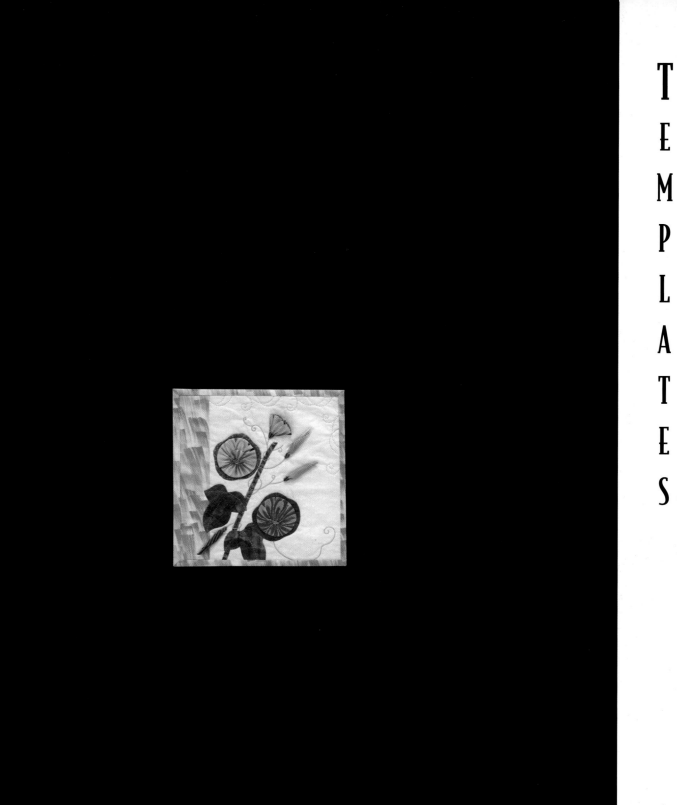

CORNFLOWER

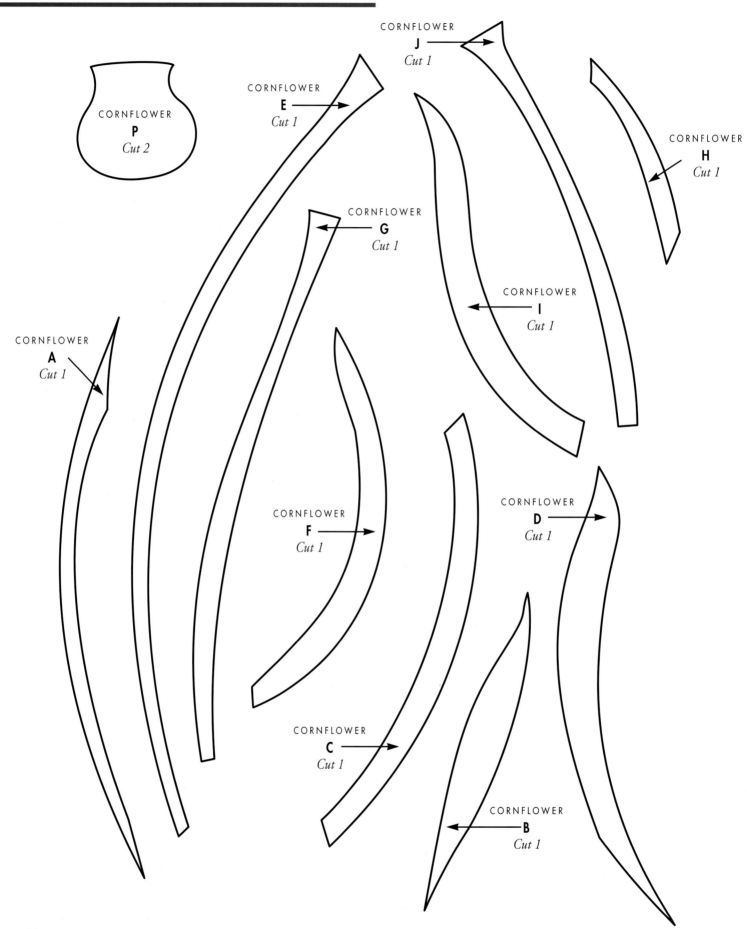

CORNFLOWER
J
Cut 1

CORNFLOWER
E
Cut 1

CORNFLOWER
H
Cut 1

CORNFLOWER
P
Cut 2

CORNFLOWER
G
Cut 1

CORNFLOWER
A
Cut 1

CORNFLOWER
I
Cut 1

CORNFLOWER
F
Cut 1

CORNFLOWER
D
Cut 1

CORNFLOWER
C
Cut 1

CORNFLOWER
B
Cut 1

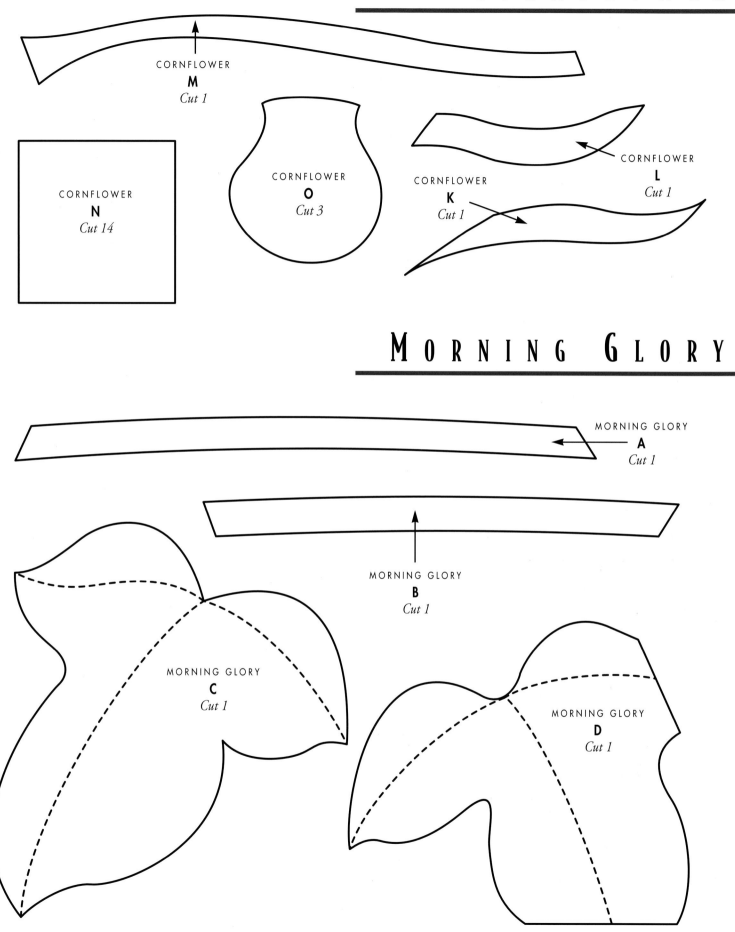

CORNFLOWER
M
Cut 1

CORNFLOWER
N
Cut 14

CORNFLOWER
O
Cut 3

CORNFLOWER
K
Cut 1

CORNFLOWER
L
Cut 1

MORNING GLORY

MORNING GLORY
A
Cut 1

MORNING GLORY
B
Cut 1

MORNING GLORY
C
Cut 1

MORNING GLORY
D
Cut 1

MORNING GLORY

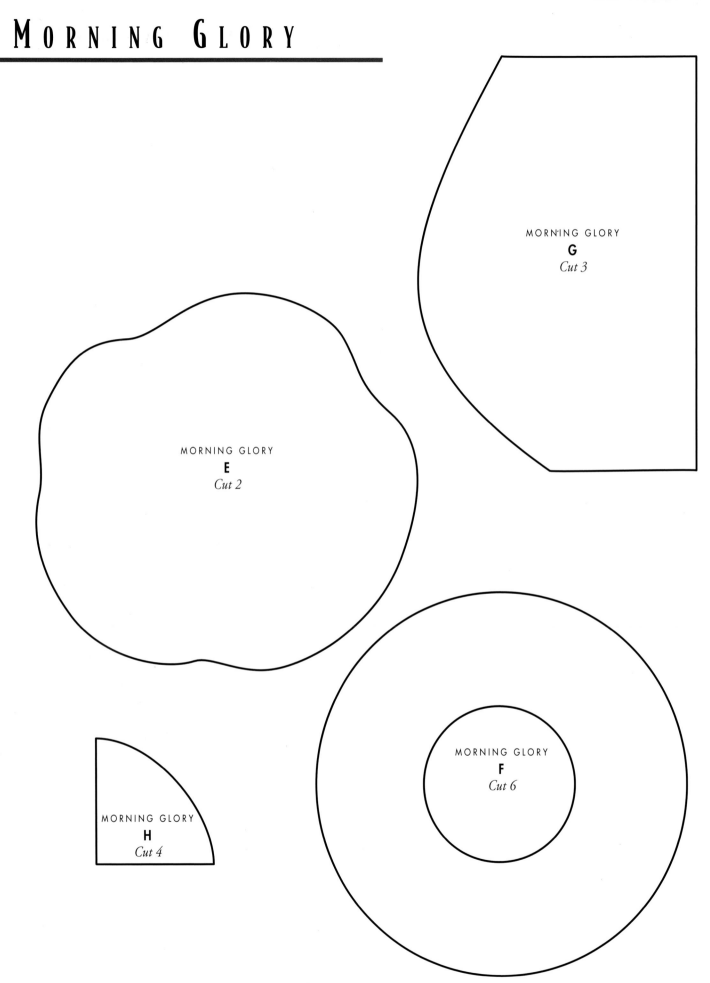

MORNING GLORY
G
Cut 3

MORNING GLORY
E
Cut 2

MORNING GLORY
F
Cut 6

MORNING GLORY
H
Cut 4

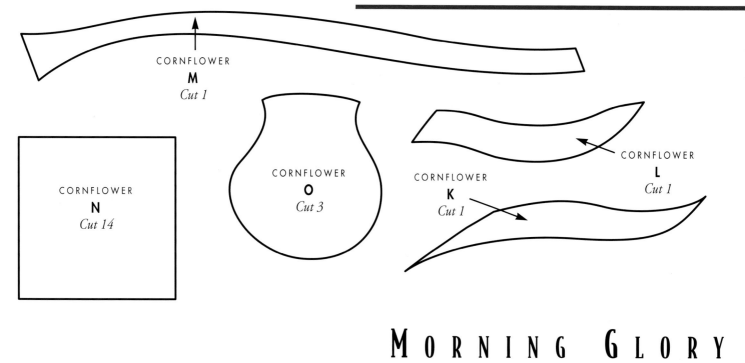

CORNFLOWER
M
Cut 1

CORNFLOWER
N
Cut 14

CORNFLOWER
O
Cut 3

CORNFLOWER
K
Cut 1

CORNFLOWER
L
Cut 1

MORNING GLORY

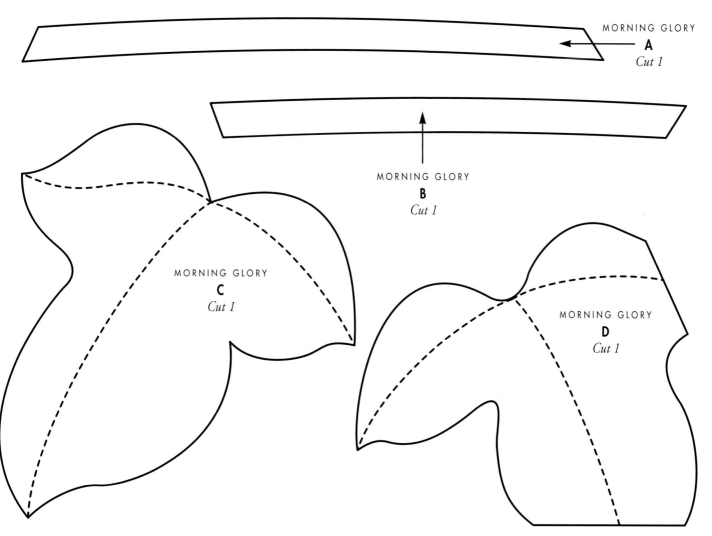

MORNING GLORY
A
Cut 1

MORNING GLORY
B
Cut 1

MORNING GLORY
C
Cut 1

MORNING GLORY
D
Cut 1

MORNING GLORY

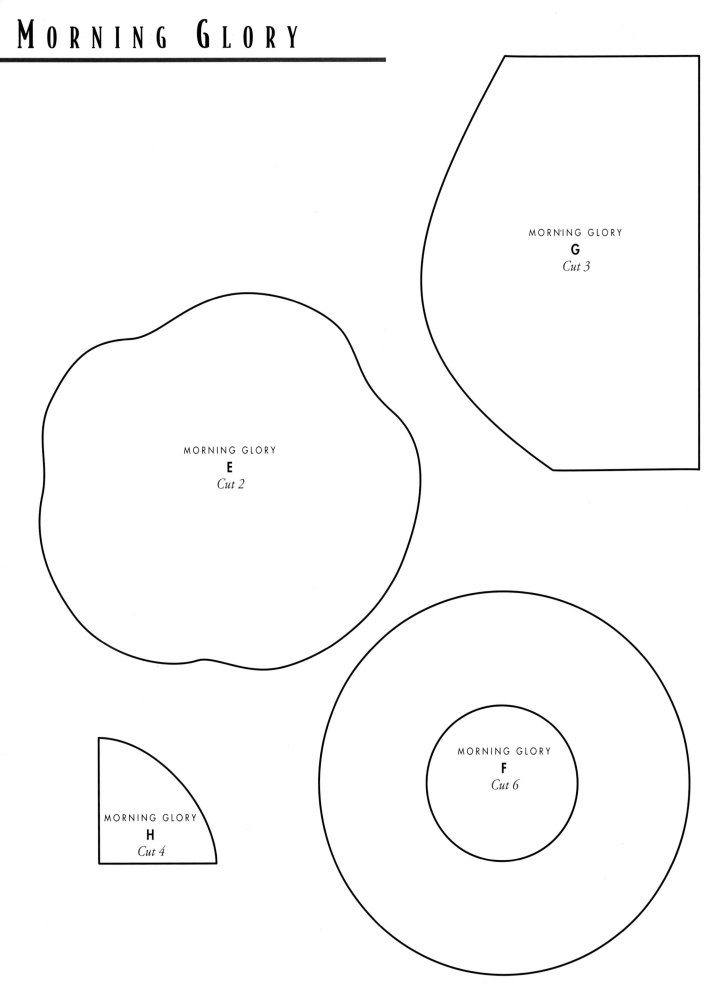

MORNING GLORY
G
Cut 3

MORNING GLORY
E
Cut 2

MORNING GLORY
H
Cut 4

MORNING GLORY
F
Cut 6

CAMELLIA JAPONICA

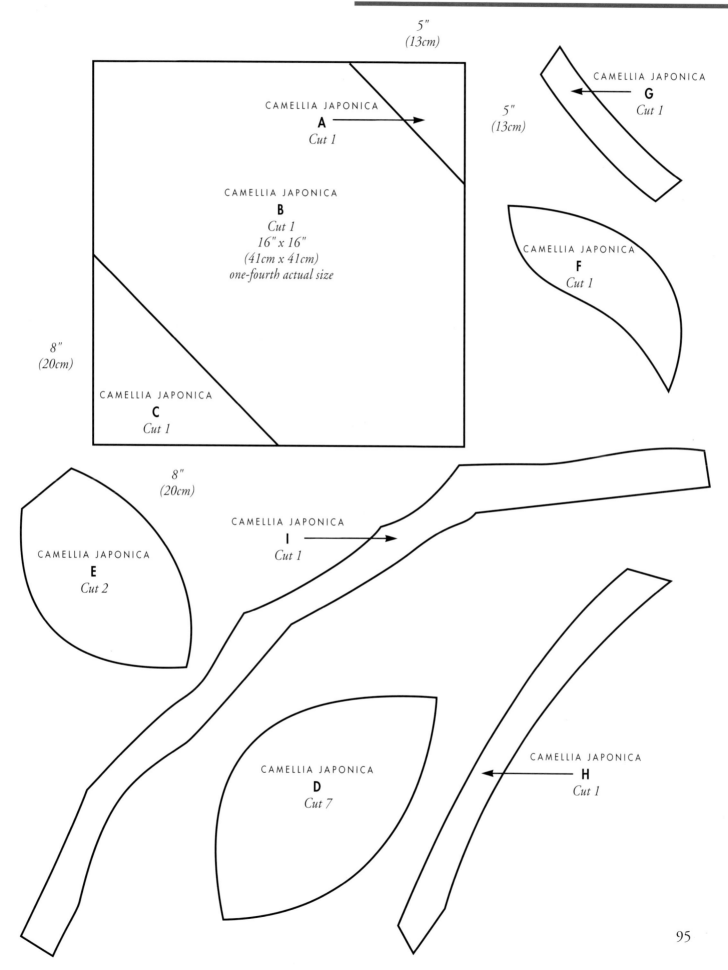

5"
(13cm)

CAMELLIA JAPONICA
A
Cut 1

5"
(13cm)

CAMELLIA JAPONICA
G
Cut 1

CAMELLIA JAPONICA
B
Cut 1
16" x 16"
(41cm x 41cm)
one-fourth actual size

CAMELLIA JAPONICA
F
Cut 1

8"
(20cm)

CAMELLIA JAPONICA
C
Cut 1

8"
(20cm)

CAMELLIA JAPONICA
I
Cut 1

CAMELLIA JAPONICA
E
Cut 2

CAMELLIA JAPONICA
H
Cut 1

CAMELLIA JAPONICA
D
Cut 7

95

CAMELLIA JAPONICA

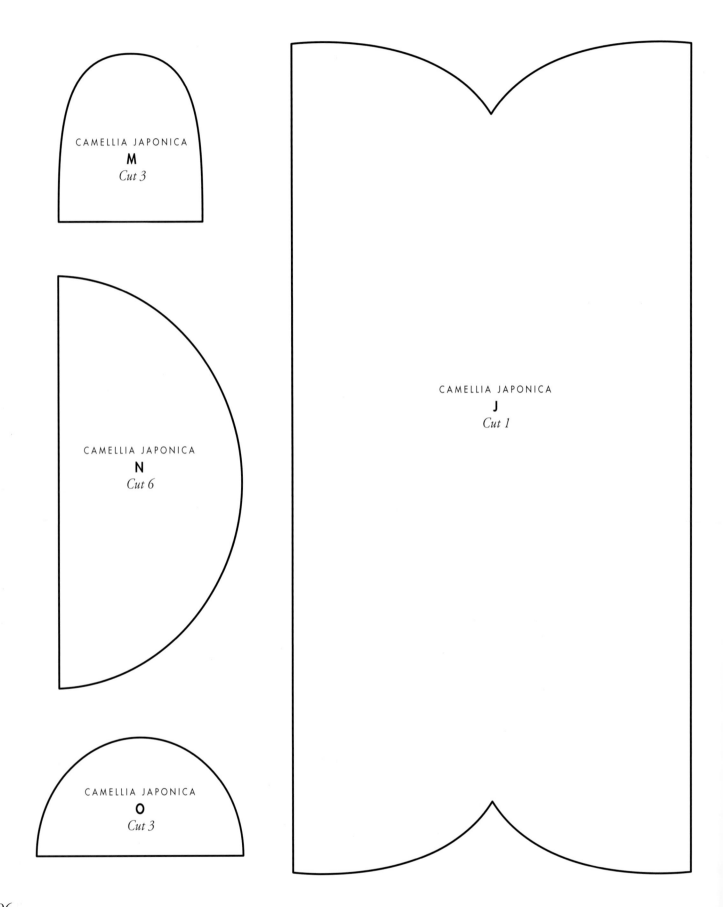

CAMELLIA JAPONICA
M
Cut 3

CAMELLIA JAPONICA
N
Cut 6

CAMELLIA JAPONICA
J
Cut 1

CAMELLIA JAPONICA
O
Cut 3

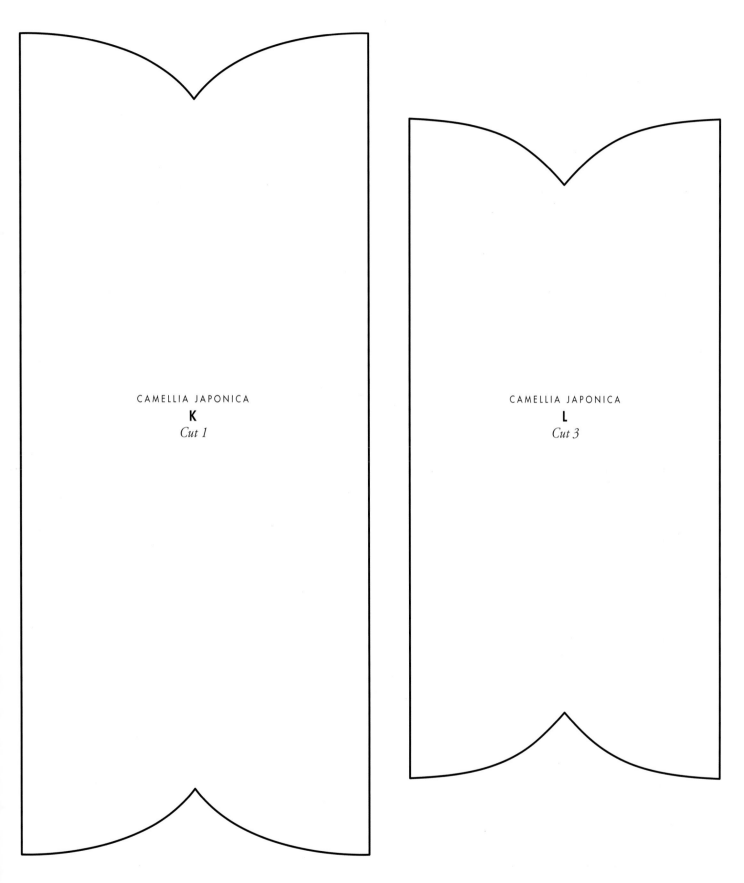

CAMELLIA JAPONICA
K
Cut 1

CAMELLIA JAPONICA
L
Cut 3

DYER'S GRAPE

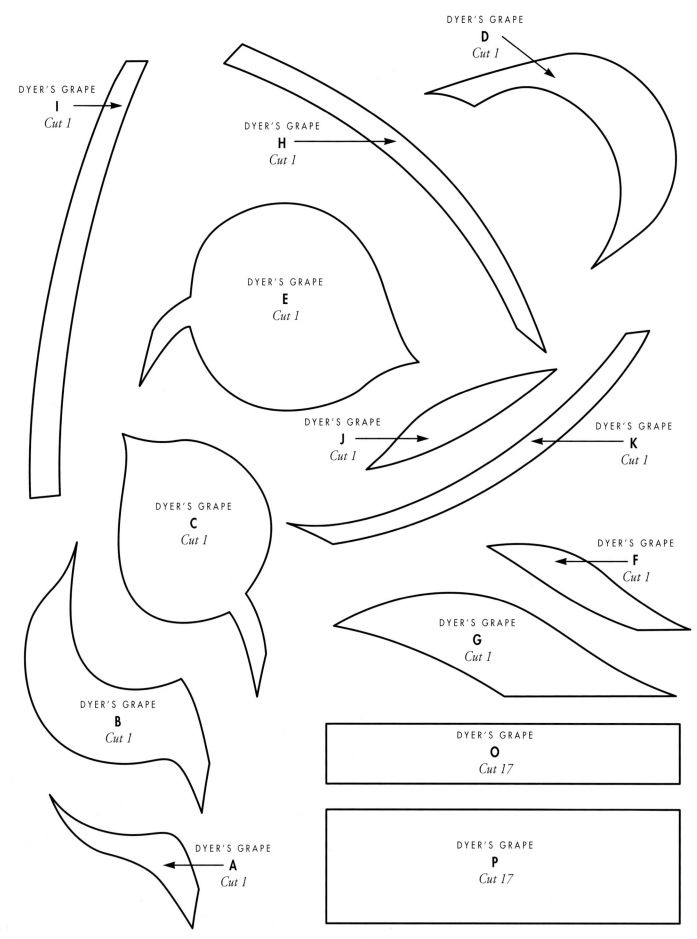

DYER'S GRAPE
I
Cut 1

DYER'S GRAPE
D
Cut 1

DYER'S GRAPE
H
Cut 1

DYER'S GRAPE
E
Cut 1

DYER'S GRAPE
J
Cut 1

DYER'S GRAPE
K
Cut 1

DYER'S GRAPE
C
Cut 1

DYER'S GRAPE
F
Cut 1

DYER'S GRAPE
G
Cut 1

DYER'S GRAPE
O
Cut 17

DYER'S GRAPE
B
Cut 1

DYER'S GRAPE
A
Cut 1

DYER'S GRAPE
P
Cut 17

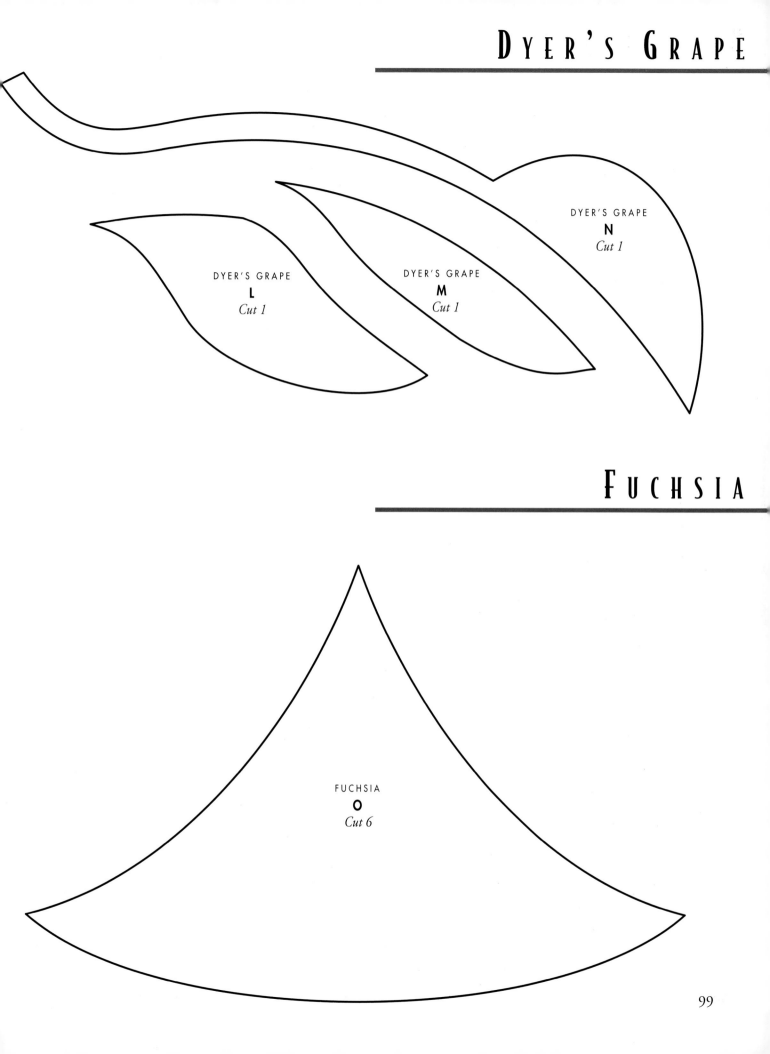

DYER'S GRAPE
N
Cut 1

DYER'S GRAPE
L
Cut 1

DYER'S GRAPE
M
Cut 1

FUCHSIA
O
Cut 6

FUCHSIA

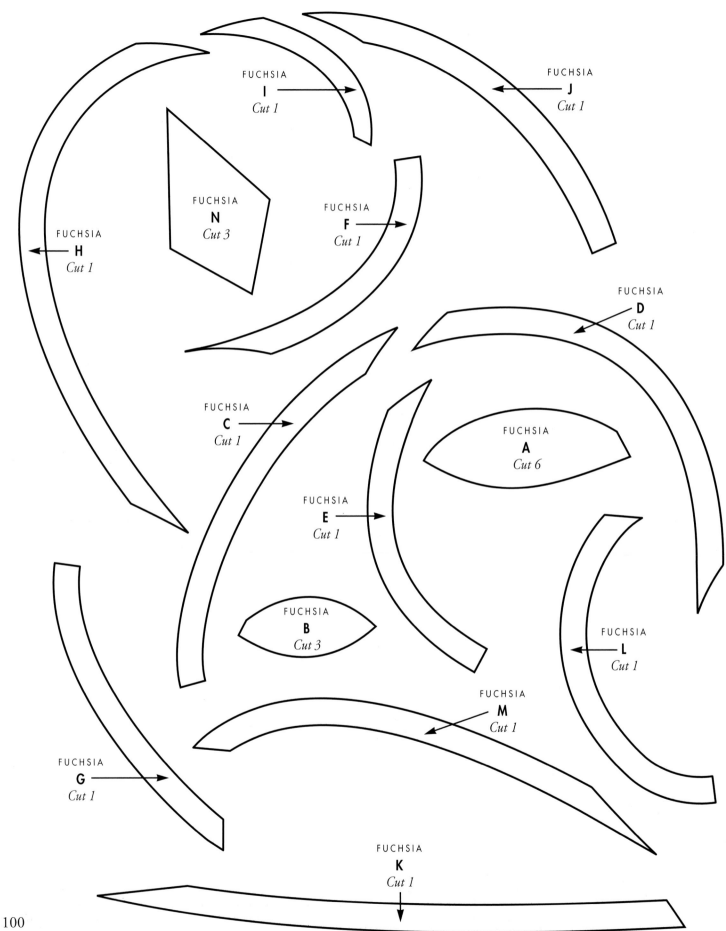

FUCHSIA
I
Cut 1

FUCHSIA
J
Cut 1

FUCHSIA
N
Cut 3

FUCHSIA
F
Cut 1

FUCHSIA
H
Cut 1

FUCHSIA
D
Cut 1

FUCHSIA
C
Cut 1

FUCHSIA
A
Cut 6

FUCHSIA
E
Cut 1

FUCHSIA
B
Cut 3

FUCHSIA
L
Cut 1

FUCHSIA
M
Cut 1

FUCHSIA
G
Cut 1

FUCHSIA
K
Cut 1

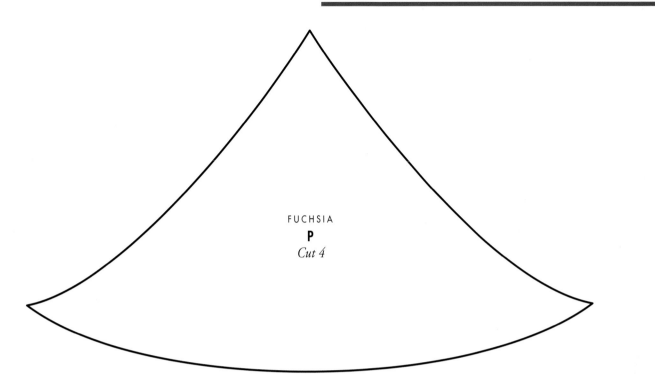

FUCHSIA
P
Cut 4

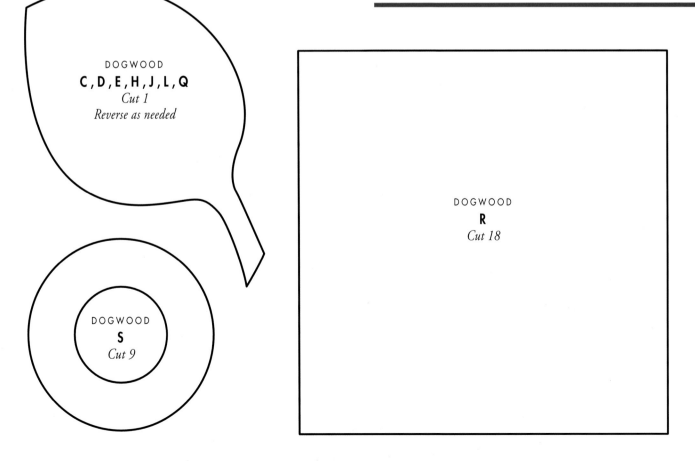

DOGWOOD
C , D , E , H , J , L , Q
Cut 1
Reverse as needed

DOGWOOD
S
Cut 9

DOGWOOD
R
Cut 18

DOGWOOD

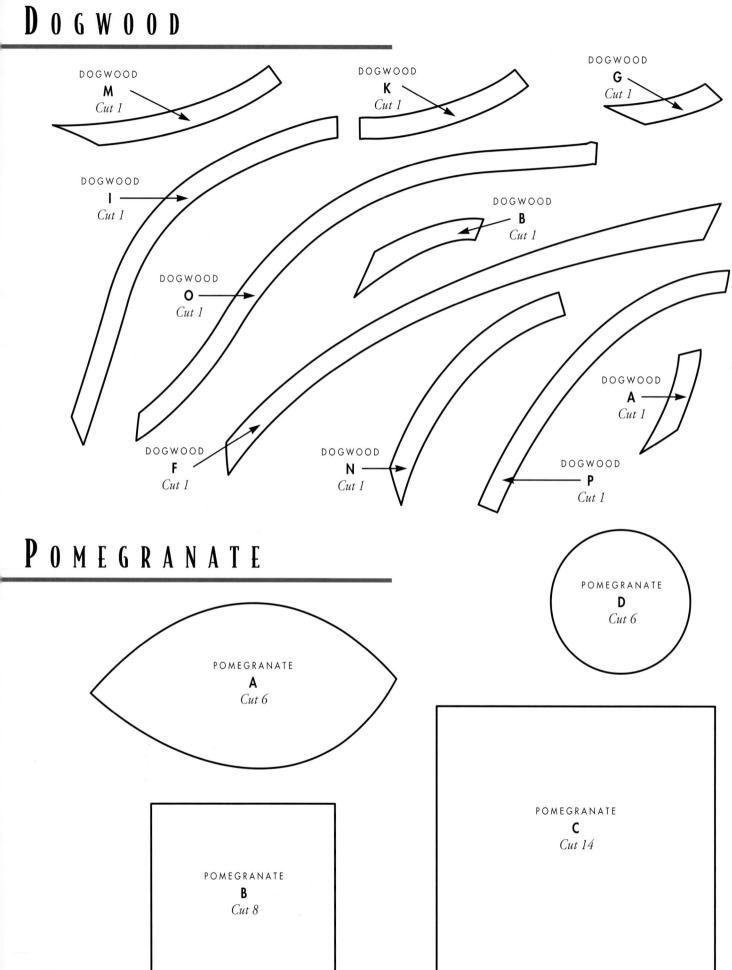

DOGWOOD
M
Cut 1

DOGWOOD
K
Cut 1

DOGWOOD
G
Cut 1

DOGWOOD
I
Cut 1

DOGWOOD
B
Cut 1

DOGWOOD
O
Cut 1

DOGWOOD
A
Cut 1

DOGWOOD
F
Cut 1

DOGWOOD
N
Cut 1

DOGWOOD
P
Cut 1

POMEGRANATE

POMEGRANATE
D
Cut 6

POMEGRANATE
A
Cut 6

POMEGRANATE
C
Cut 14

POMEGRANATE
B
Cut 8

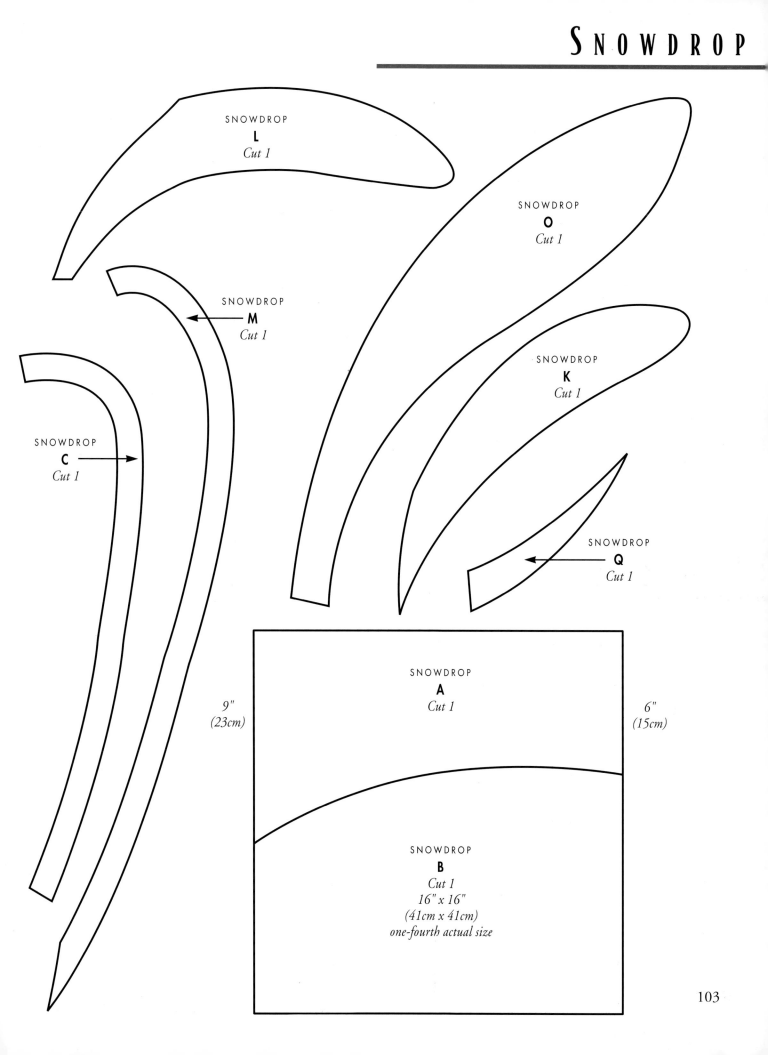

SNOWDROP
L
Cut 1

SNOWDROP
O
Cut 1

SNOWDROP
M
Cut 1

SNOWDROP
K
Cut 1

SNOWDROP
C
Cut 1

SNOWDROP
Q
Cut 1

9"
(23cm)

6"
(15cm)

SNOWDROP
A
Cut 1

SNOWDROP
B
Cut 1
16" x 16"
(41cm x 41cm)
one-fourth actual size

SNOWDROP

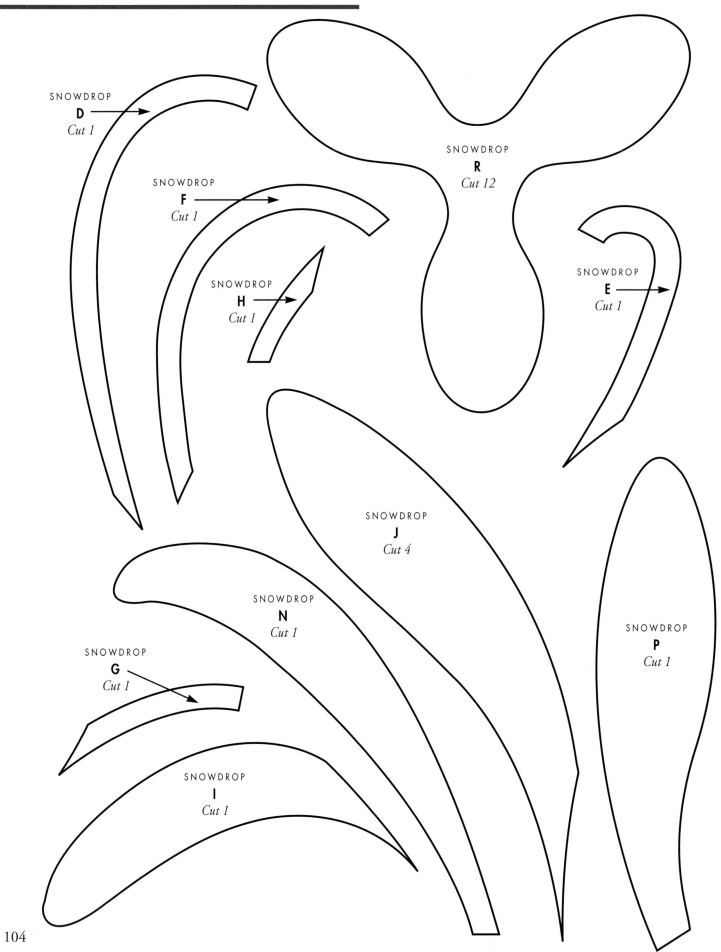

SNOWDROP
D
Cut 1

SNOWDROP
F
Cut 1

SNOWDROP
H
Cut 1

SNOWDROP
R
Cut 12

SNOWDROP
E
Cut 1

SNOWDROP
J
Cut 4

SNOWDROP
N
Cut 1

SNOWDROP
P
Cut 1

SNOWDROP
G
Cut 1

SNOWDROP
I
Cut 1

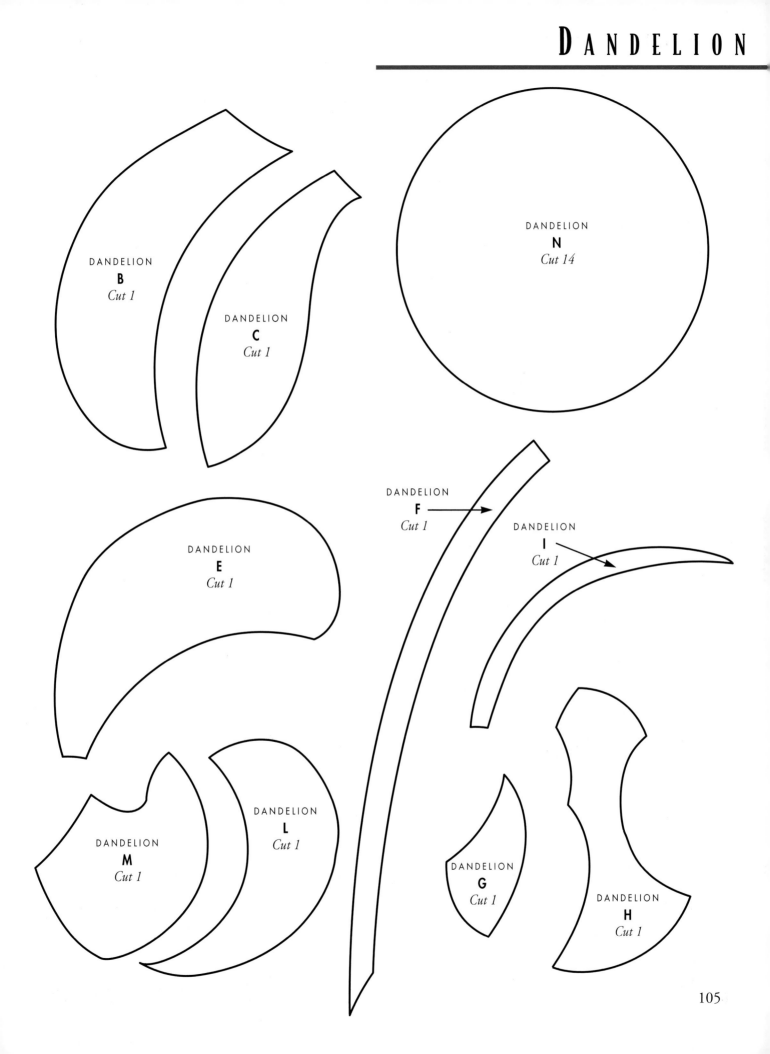

DANDELION
B
Cut 1

DANDELION
C
Cut 1

DANDELION
N
Cut 14

DANDELION
E
Cut 1

DANDELION
F
Cut 1

DANDELION
I
Cut 1

DANDELION
M
Cut 1

DANDELION
L
Cut 1

DANDELION
G
Cut 1

DANDELION
H
Cut 1

DANDELION

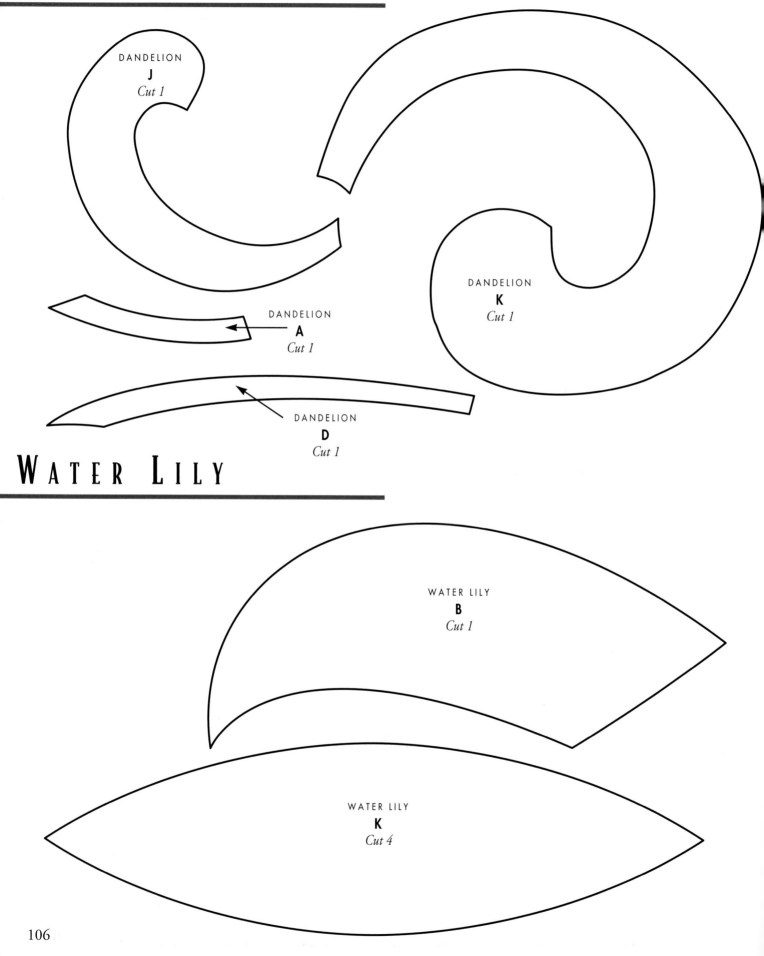

DANDELION
J
Cut 1

DANDELION
K
Cut 1

DANDELION
A
Cut 1

DANDELION
D
Cut 1

WATER LILY

WATER LILY
B
Cut 1

WATER LILY
K
Cut 4

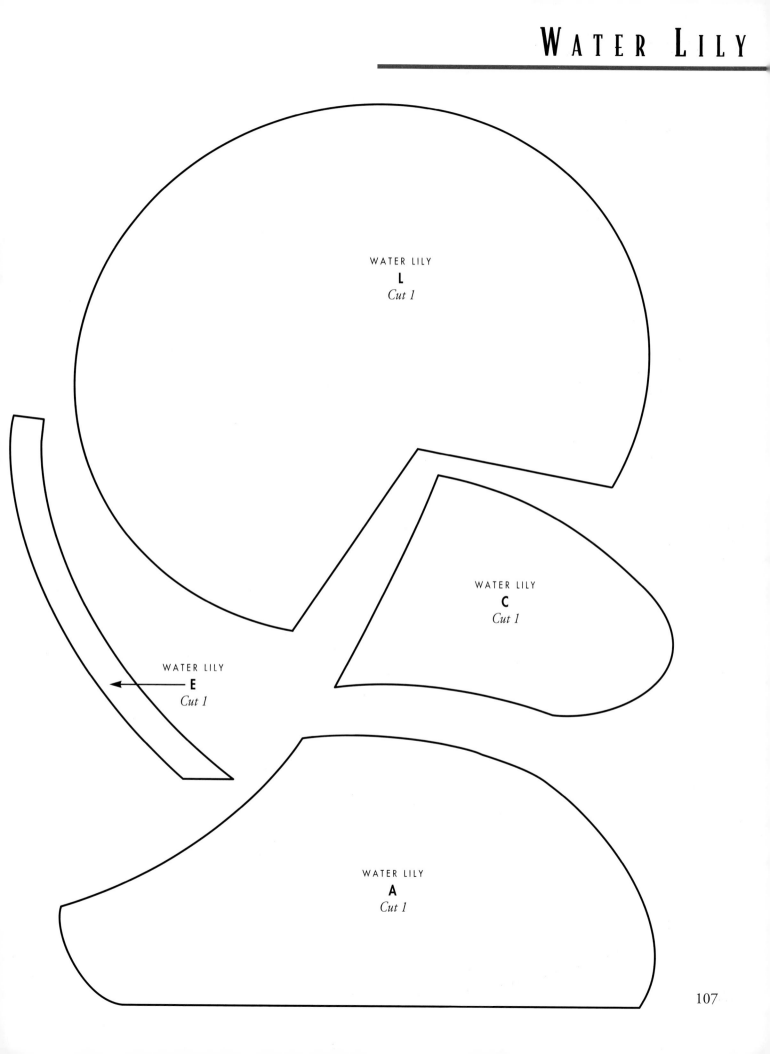

WATER LILY
L
Cut 1

WATER LILY
C
Cut 1

WATER LILY
E
Cut 1

WATER LILY
A
Cut 1

Water Lily

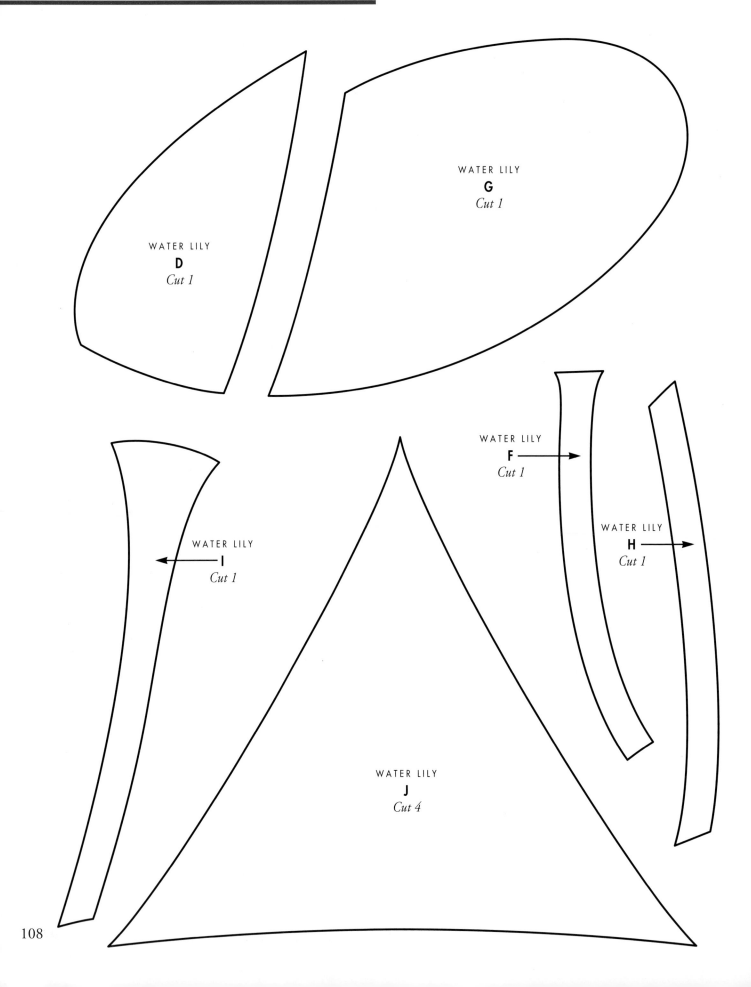

WATER LILY
G
Cut 1

WATER LILY
D
Cut 1

WATER LILY
F ⟶
Cut 1

WATER LILY
H ⟶
Cut 1

WATER LILY
⟵ **I**
Cut 1

WATER LILY
J
Cut 4

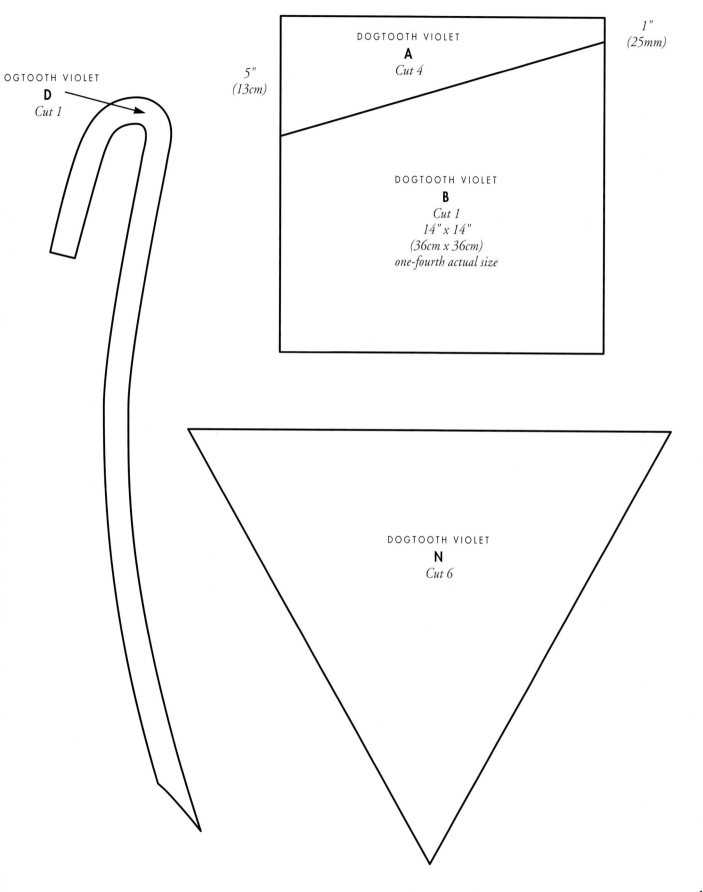

OGTOOTH VIOLET

D

Cut 1

DOGTOOTH VIOLET

A

Cut 4

5"
(13cm)

1"
(25mm)

DOGTOOTH VIOLET

B

Cut 1
14" x 14"
(36cm x 36cm)
one-fourth actual size

DOGTOOTH VIOLET

N

Cut 6

DOGTOOTH VIOLET

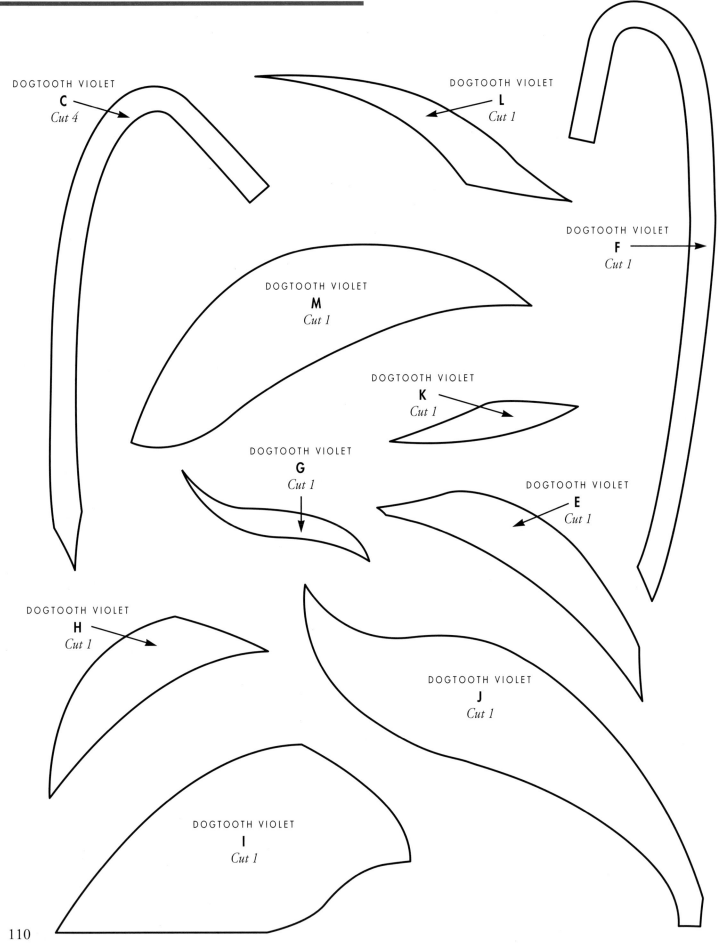

DOGTOOTH VIOLET

C

Cut 4

DOGTOOTH VIOLET

L

Cut 1

DOGTOOTH VIOLET

F

Cut 1

DOGTOOTH VIOLET

M

Cut 1

DOGTOOTH VIOLET

K

Cut 1

DOGTOOTH VIOLET

G

Cut 1

DOGTOOTH VIOLET

E

Cut 1

DOGTOOTH VIOLET

H

Cut 1

DOGTOOTH VIOLET

J

Cut 1

DOGTOOTH VIOLET

I

Cut 1

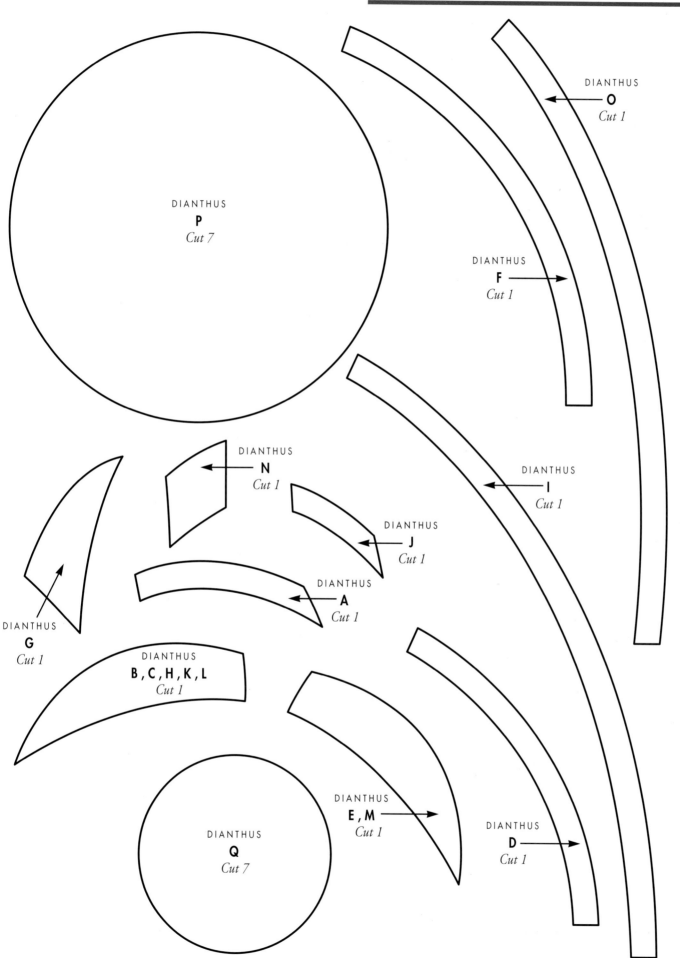

DIANTHUS
O
Cut 1

DIANTHUS
P
Cut 7

DIANTHUS
F
Cut 1

DIANTHUS
N
Cut 1

DIANTHUS
I
Cut 1

DIANTHUS
J
Cut 1

DIANTHUS
A
Cut 1

DIANTHUS
G
Cut 1

DIANTHUS
B, C, H, K, L
Cut 1

DIANTHUS
Q
Cut 7

DIANTHUS
E, M
Cut 1

DIANTHUS
D
Cut 1

AKEBIA

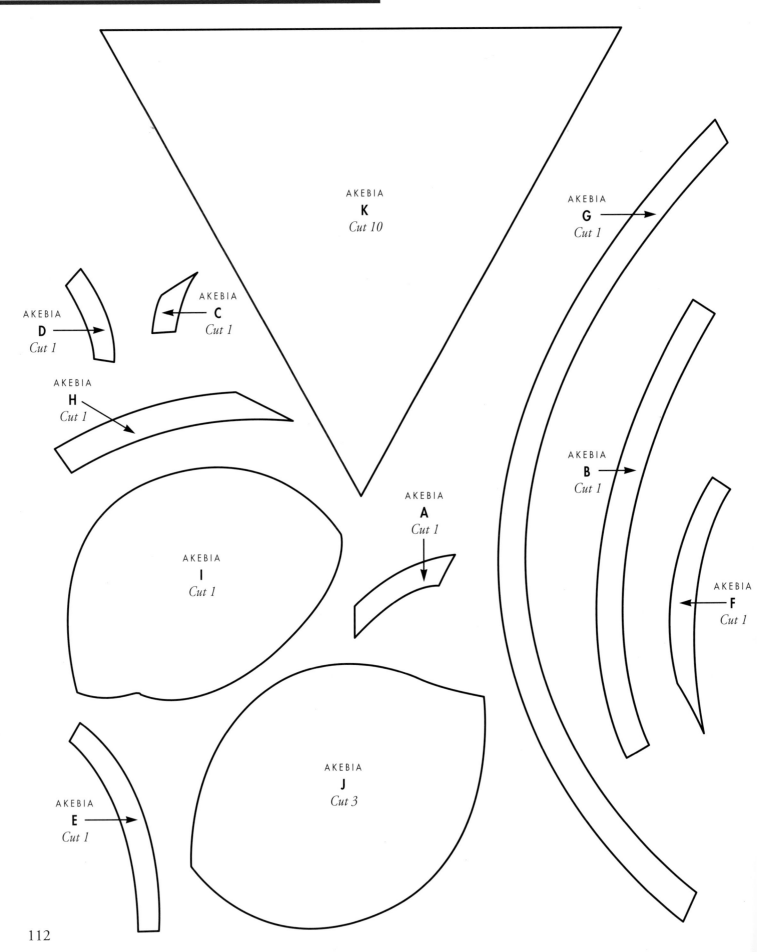

AKEBIA
K
Cut 10

AKEBIA
G
Cut 1

AKEBIA
D
Cut 1

AKEBIA
C
Cut 1

AKEBIA
H
Cut 1

AKEBIA
B
Cut 1

AKEBIA
A
Cut 1

AKEBIA
I
Cut 1

AKEBIA
F
Cut 1

AKEBIA
J
Cut 3

AKEBIA
E
Cut 1

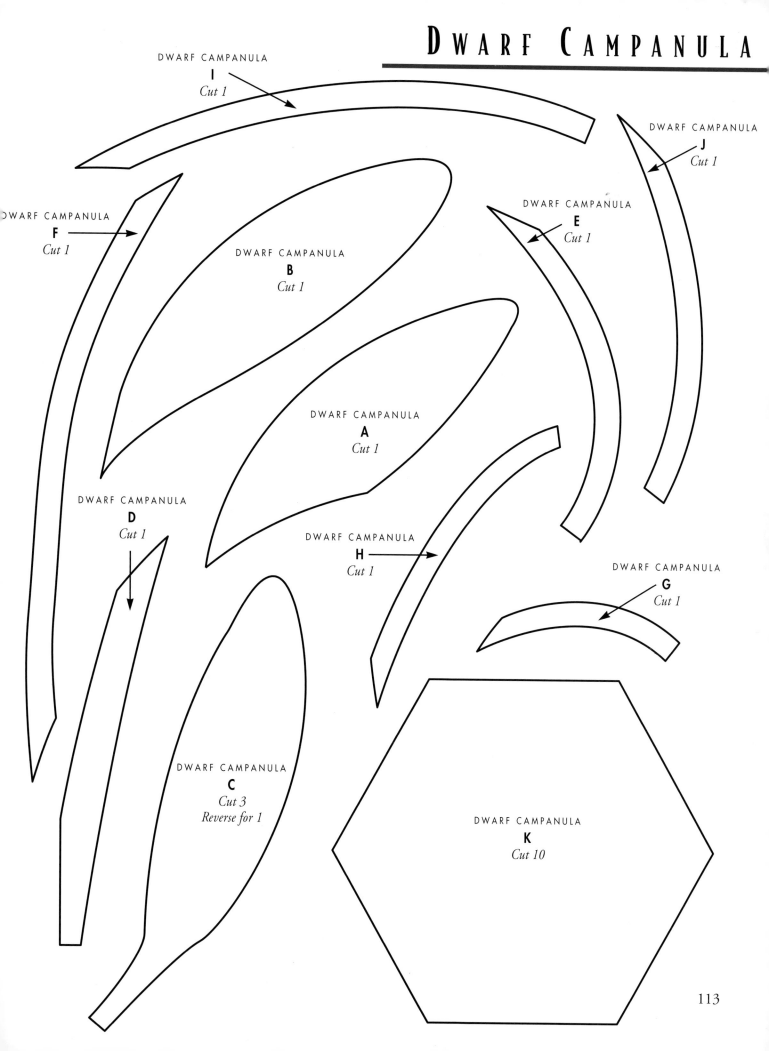

DWARF CAMPANULA

DWARF CAMPANULA
I
Cut 1

DWARF CAMPANULA
J
Cut 1

DWARF CAMPANULA
F
Cut 1

DWARF CAMPANULA
B
Cut 1

DWARF CAMPANULA
E
Cut 1

DWARF CAMPANULA
A
Cut 1

DWARF CAMPANULA
D
Cut 1

DWARF CAMPANULA
H
Cut 1

DWARF CAMPANULA
G
Cut 1

DWARF CAMPANULA
C
Cut 3
Reverse for 1

DWARF CAMPANULA
K
Cut 10

113

POPPY

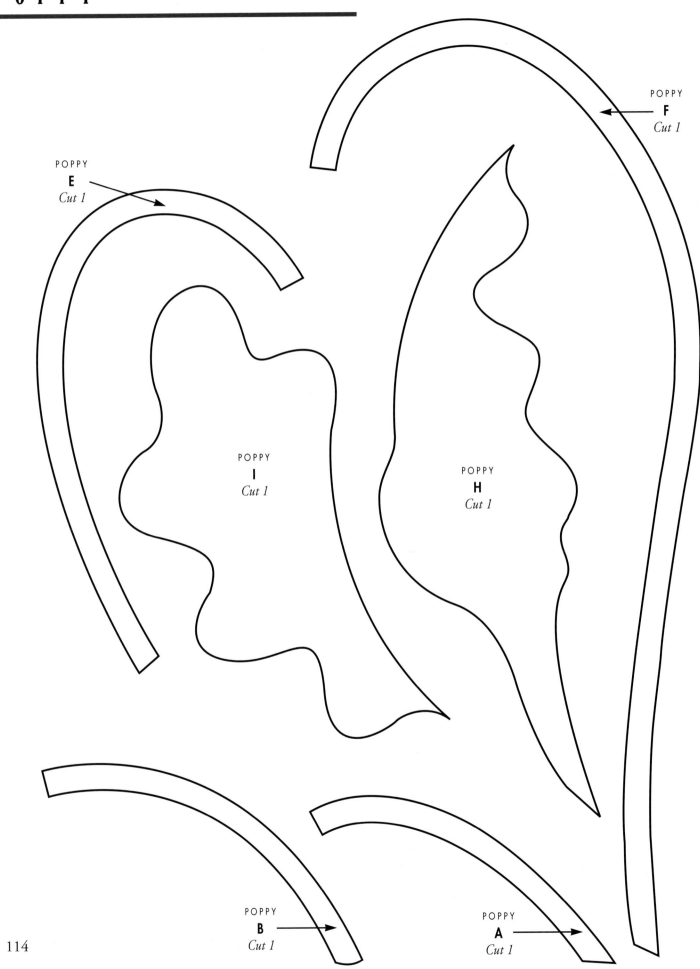

POPPY
F
Cut 1

POPPY
E
Cut 1

POPPY
I
Cut 1

POPPY
H
Cut 1

POPPY
B
Cut 1

POPPY
A
Cut 1

114

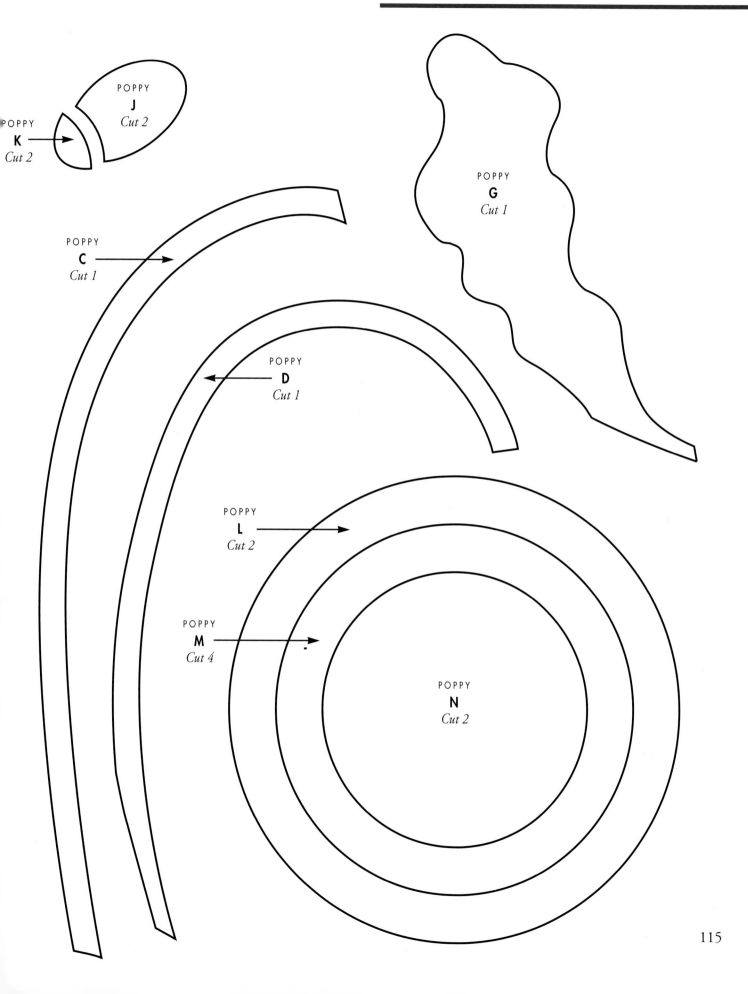

POPPY
J
Cut 2

POPPY
K
Cut 2

POPPY
G
Cut 1

POPPY
C
Cut 1

POPPY
D
Cut 1

POPPY
L
Cut 2

POPPY
M
Cut 4

POPPY
N
Cut 2

BOTTLE GOURD

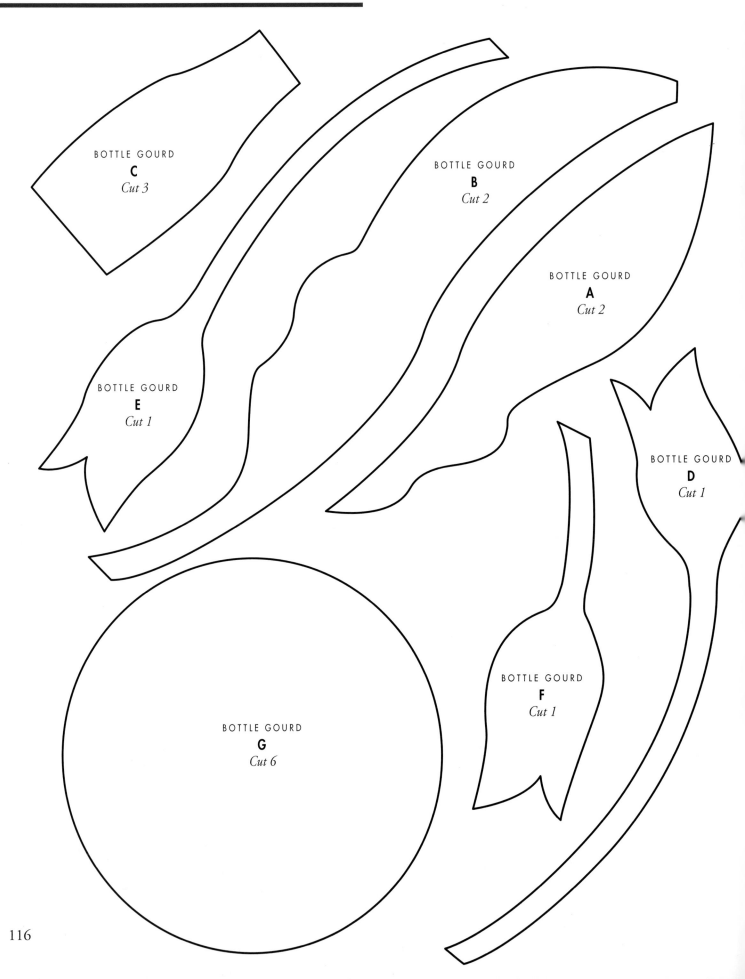

BOTTLE GOURD
C
Cut 3

BOTTLE GOURD
B
Cut 2

BOTTLE GOURD
A
Cut 2

BOTTLE GOURD
E
Cut 1

BOTTLE GOURD
D
Cut 1

BOTTLE GOURD
F
Cut 1

BOTTLE GOURD
G
Cut 6

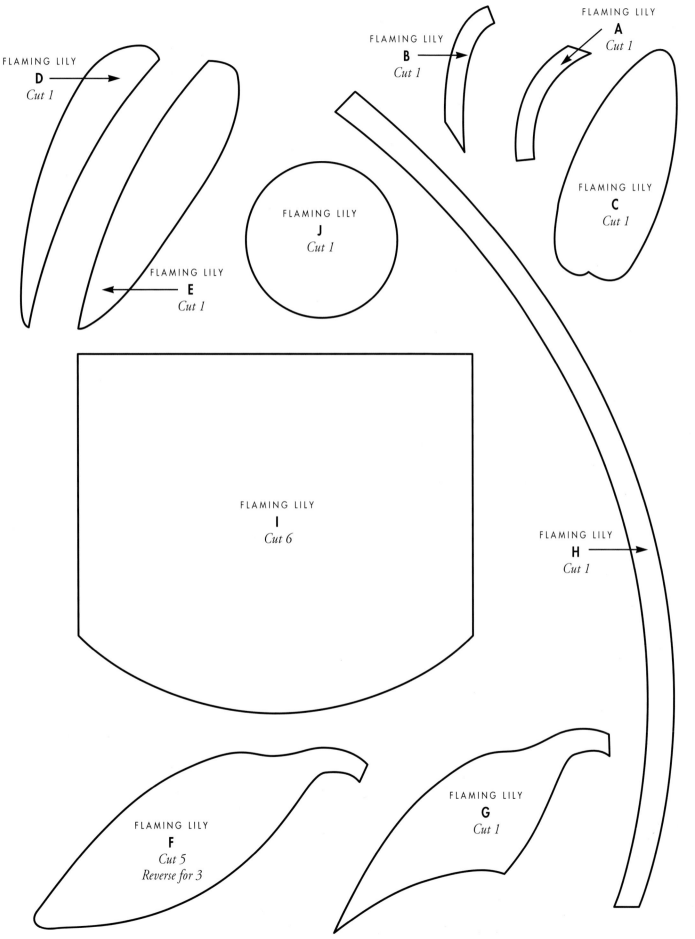

FLAMING LILY
D
Cut 1

FLAMING LILY
B
Cut 1

FLAMING LILY
A
Cut 1

FLAMING LILY
C
Cut 1

FLAMING LILY
J
Cut 1

FLAMING LILY
E
Cut 1

FLAMING LILY
I
Cut 6

FLAMING LILY
H
Cut 1

FLAMING LILY
F
Cut 5
Reverse for 3

FLAMING LILY
G
Cut 1

117

BINDWEED

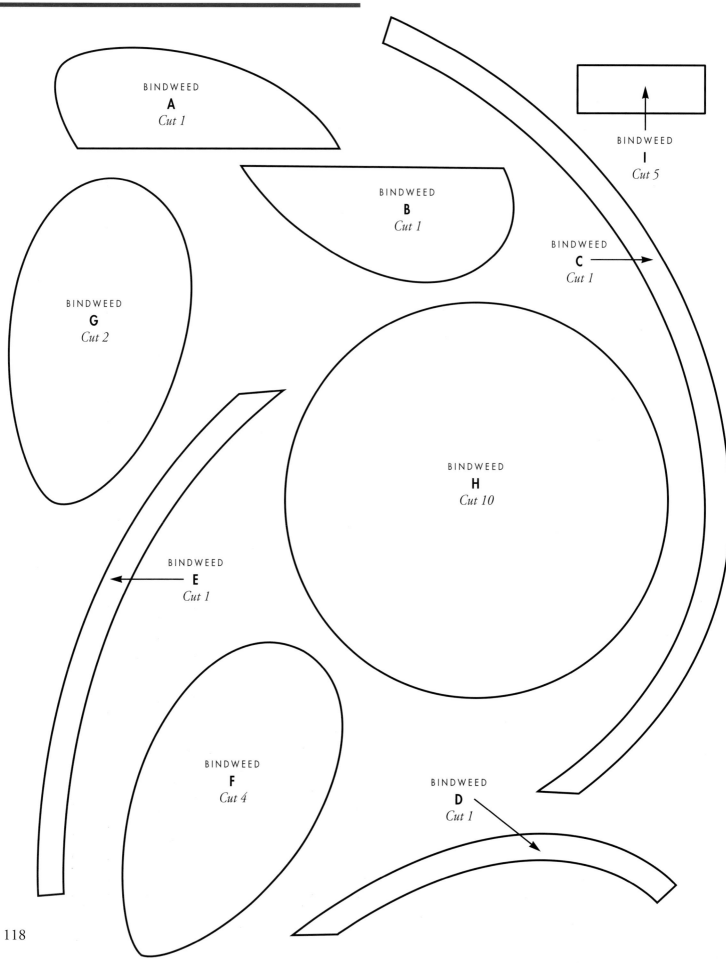

BINDWEED
A
Cut 1

BINDWEED
B
Cut 1

BINDWEED
I
Cut 5

BINDWEED
C
Cut 1

BINDWEED
G
Cut 2

BINDWEED
H
Cut 10

BINDWEED
E
Cut 1

BINDWEED
F
Cut 4

BINDWEED
D
Cut 1

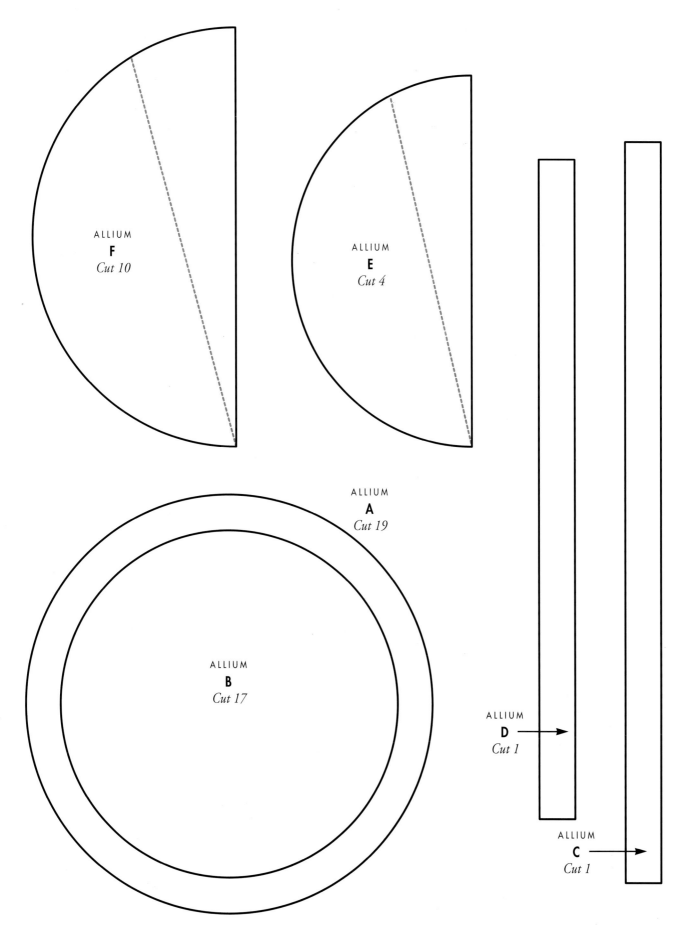

ALLIUM
F
Cut 10

ALLIUM
E
Cut 4

ALLIUM
A
Cut 19

ALLIUM
B
Cut 17

ALLIUM
D
Cut 1

ALLIUM
C
Cut 1

FOUNTAIN PLANT

FOUNTAIN PLANT
B
Cut 5
Reverse for 2

FOUNTAIN PLANT
A
Cut 1

FOUNTAIN PLANT
H
Cut 9

FOUNTAIN
PLANT
G
Cut 6

FOUNTAIN PLANT
F
Cut 9

FOUNTAIN PLANT
E
Cut 1

FOUNTAIN PLANT
D
Cut 1

FOUNTAIN PLANT
C
Cut 1

LILY OF THE VALLEY

LILY OF
THE VALLEY
B
Cut 1

LILY OF
THE VALLEY
L
Cut 1

LILY OF
THE VALLEY
J
Cut 1

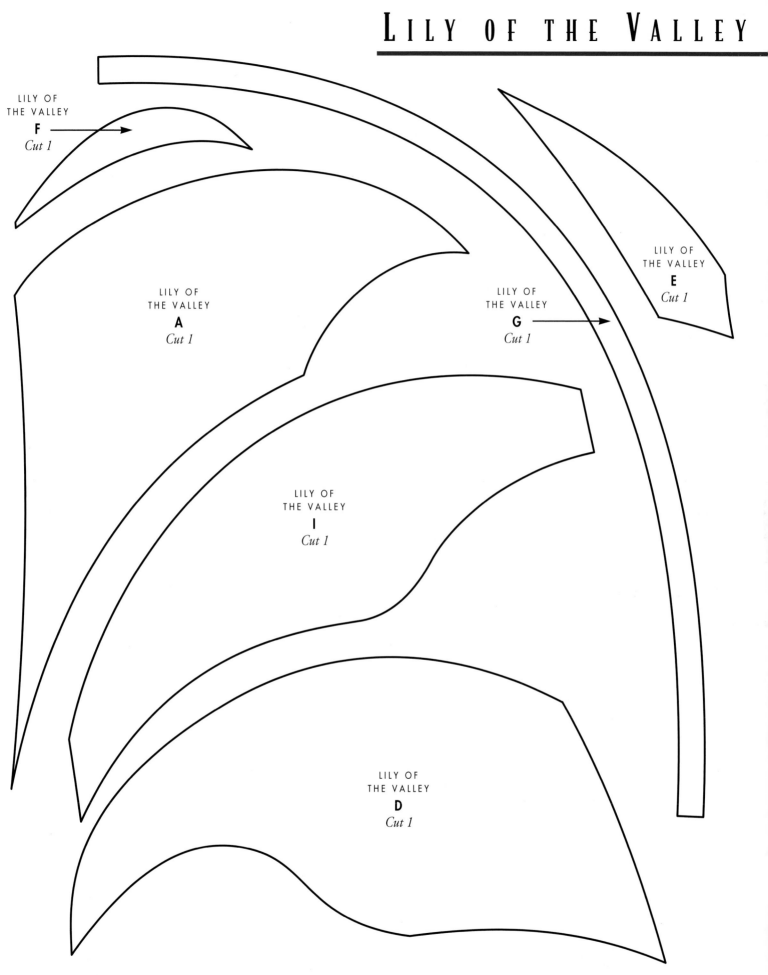

LILY OF
THE VALLEY

F

Cut 1

LILY OF
THE VALLEY

A

Cut 1

LILY OF
THE VALLEY

G

Cut 1

LILY OF
THE VALLEY

E

Cut 1

LILY OF
THE VALLEY

I

Cut 1

LILY OF
THE VALLEY

D

Cut 1

121

LILY OF THE VALLEY

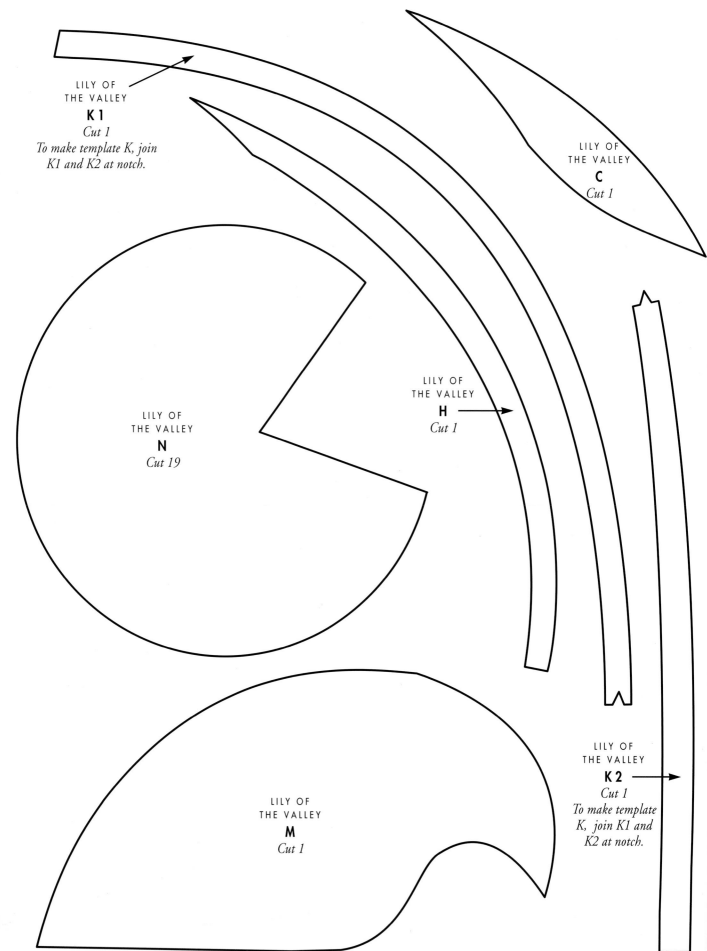

LILY OF
THE VALLEY

K1

Cut 1

*To make template K, join
K1 and K2 at notch.*

LILY OF
THE VALLEY

C

Cut 1

LILY OF
THE VALLEY

N

Cut 19

LILY OF
THE VALLEY

H

Cut 1

LILY OF
THE VALLEY

K2

Cut 1

*To make template
K, join K1 and
K2 at notch.*

LILY OF
THE VALLEY

M

Cut 1

122

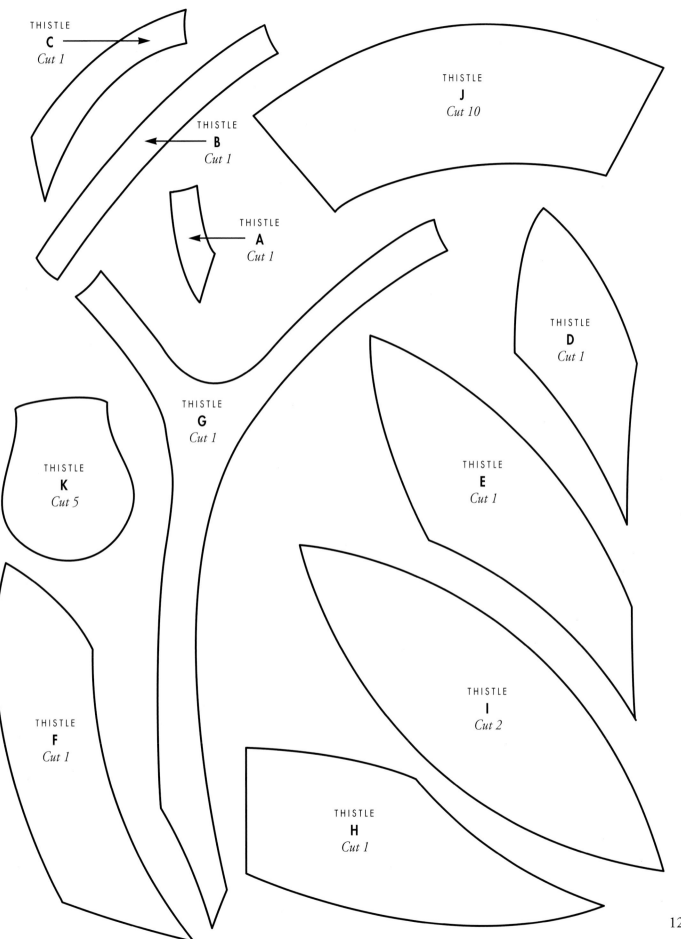

THISTLE
C
Cut 1

THISTLE
B
Cut 1

THISTLE
J
Cut 10

THISTLE
A
Cut 1

THISTLE
D
Cut 1

THISTLE
G
Cut 1

THISTLE
K
Cut 5

THISTLE
E
Cut 1

THISTLE
F
Cut 1

THISTLE
I
Cut 2

THISTLE
H
Cut 1

CLEMATIS

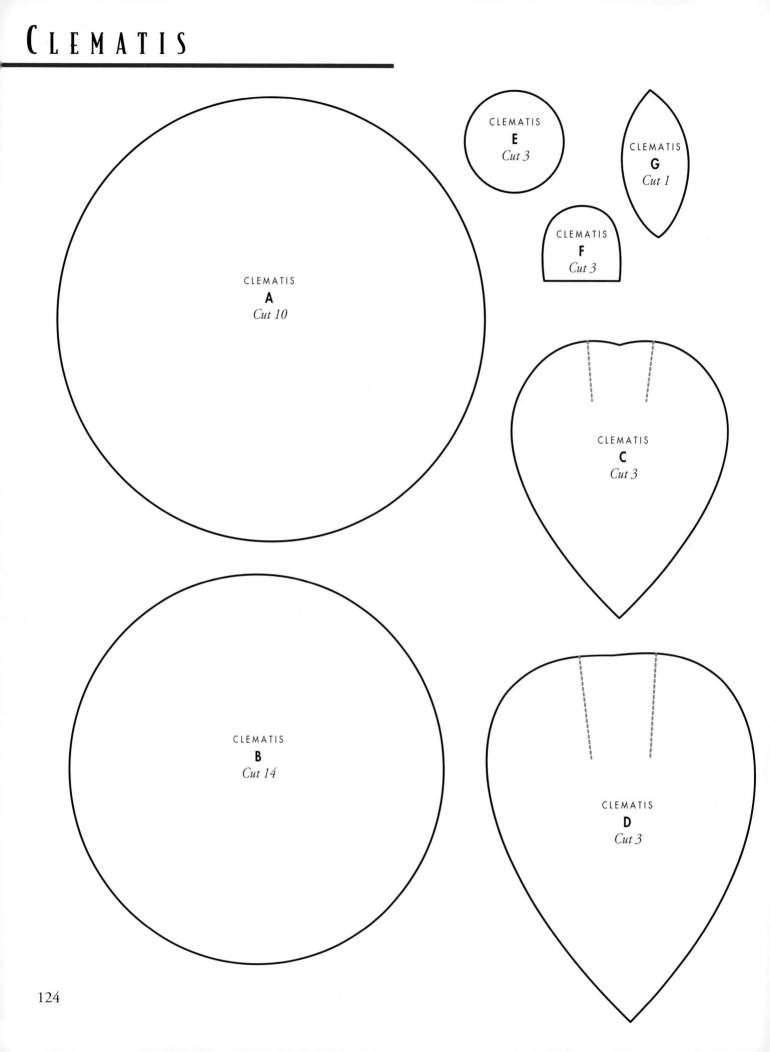

CLEMATIS
E
Cut 3

CLEMATIS
G
Cut 1

CLEMATIS
F
Cut 3

CLEMATIS
A
Cut 10

CLEMATIS
C
Cut 3

CLEMATIS
B
Cut 14

CLEMATIS
D
Cut 3

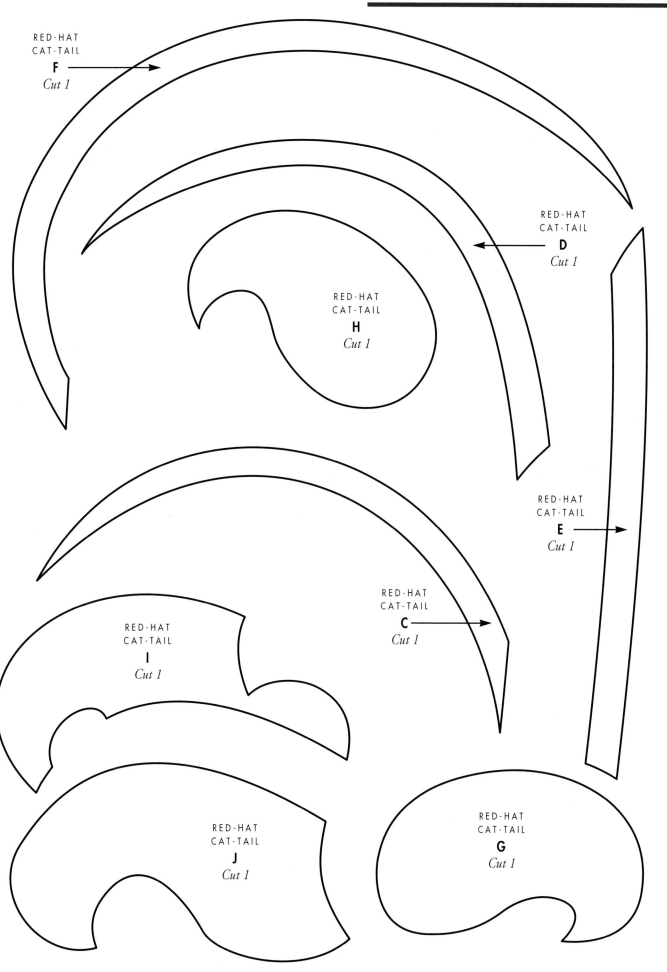

RED-HAT
CAT-TAIL
F
Cut 1

RED-HAT
CAT-TAIL
D
Cut 1

RED-HAT
CAT-TAIL
H
Cut 1

RED-HAT
CAT-TAIL
E
Cut 1

RED-HAT
CAT-TAIL
C
Cut 1

RED-HAT
CAT-TAIL
I
Cut 1

RED-HAT
CAT-TAIL
J
Cut 1

RED-HAT
CAT-TAIL
G
Cut 1

125

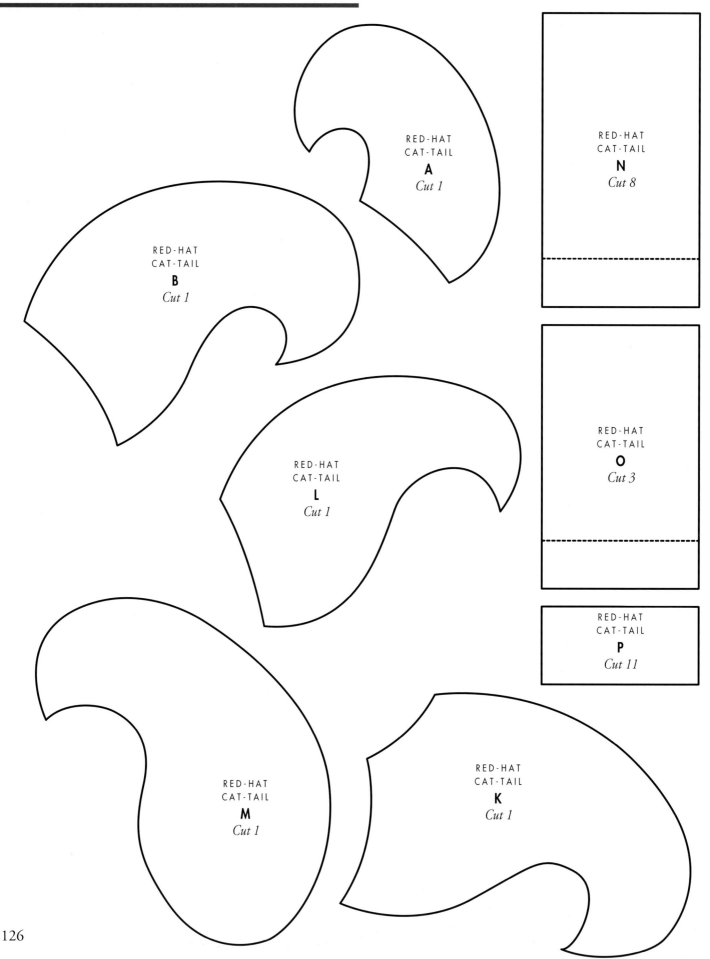

RED-HAT
CAT-TAIL
A
Cut 1

RED-HAT
CAT-TAIL
N
Cut 8

RED-HAT
CAT-TAIL
B
Cut 1

RED-HAT
CAT-TAIL
L
Cut 1

RED-HAT
CAT-TAIL
O
Cut 3

RED-HAT
CAT-TAIL
P
Cut 11

RED-HAT
CAT-TAIL
M
Cut 1

RED-HAT
CAT-TAIL
K
Cut 1

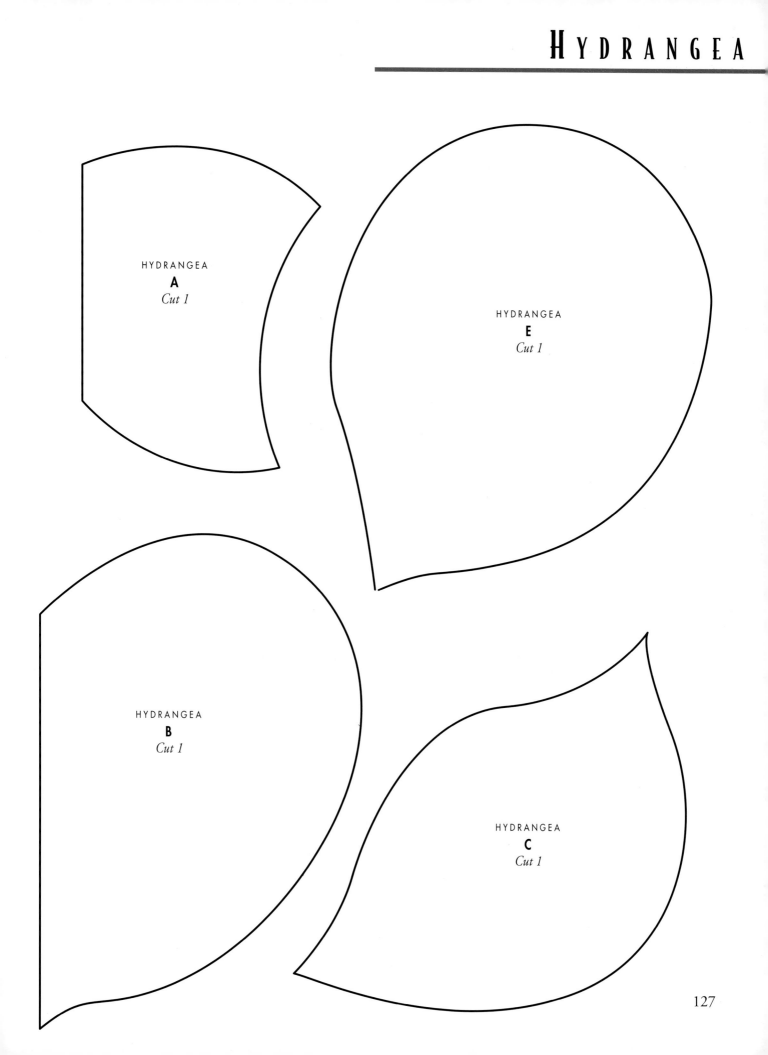

HYDRANGEA
A
Cut 1

HYDRANGEA
E
Cut 1

HYDRANGEA
B
Cut 1

HYDRANGEA
C
Cut 1

H YDRANGEA

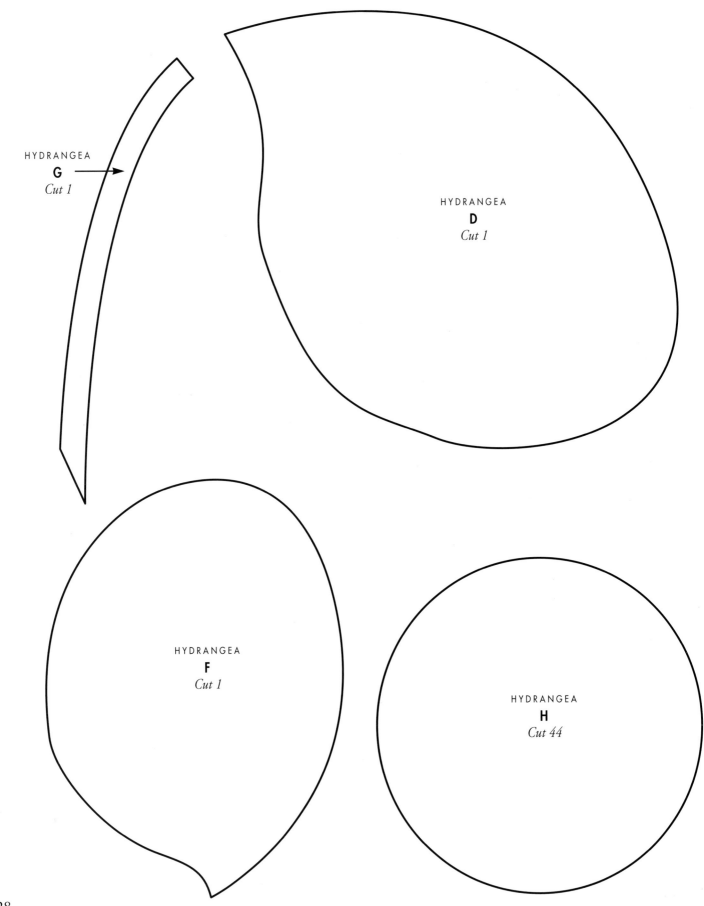

HYDRANGEA
G
Cut 1

HYDRANGEA
D
Cut 1

HYDRANGEA
F
Cut 1

HYDRANGEA
H
Cut 44

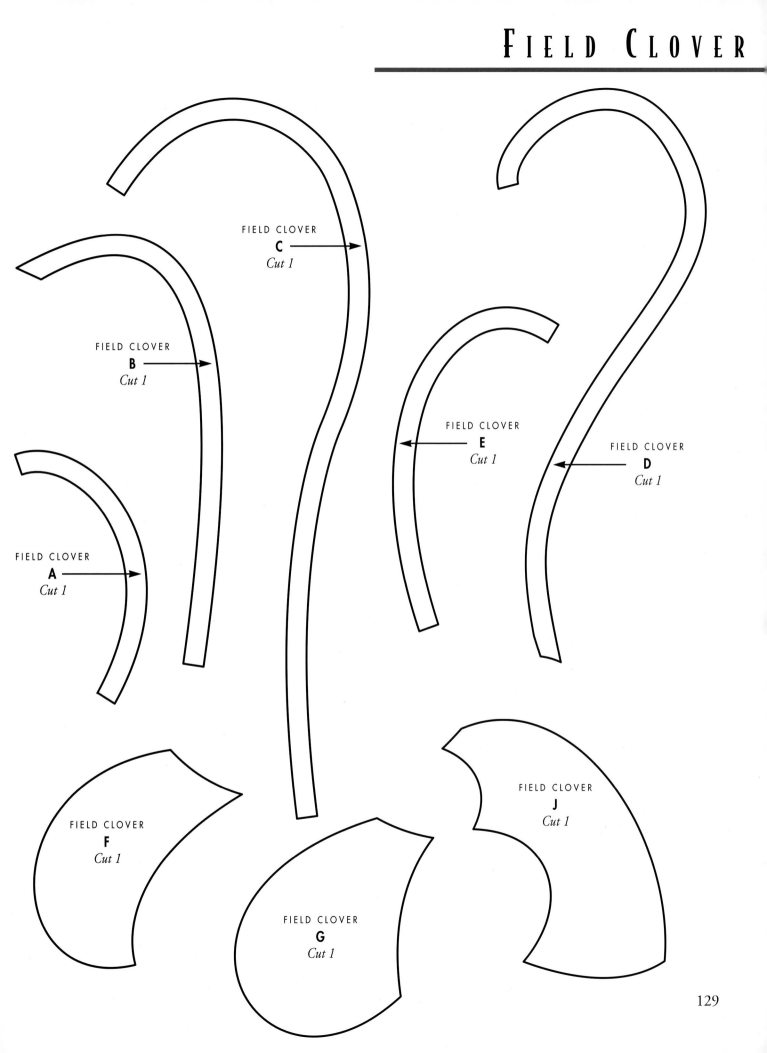

FIELD CLOVER
C
Cut 1

FIELD CLOVER
B
Cut 1

FIELD CLOVER
E
Cut 1

FIELD CLOVER
D
Cut 1

FIELD CLOVER
A
Cut 1

FIELD CLOVER
F
Cut 1

FIELD CLOVER
G
Cut 1

FIELD CLOVER
J
Cut 1

FIELD CLOVER

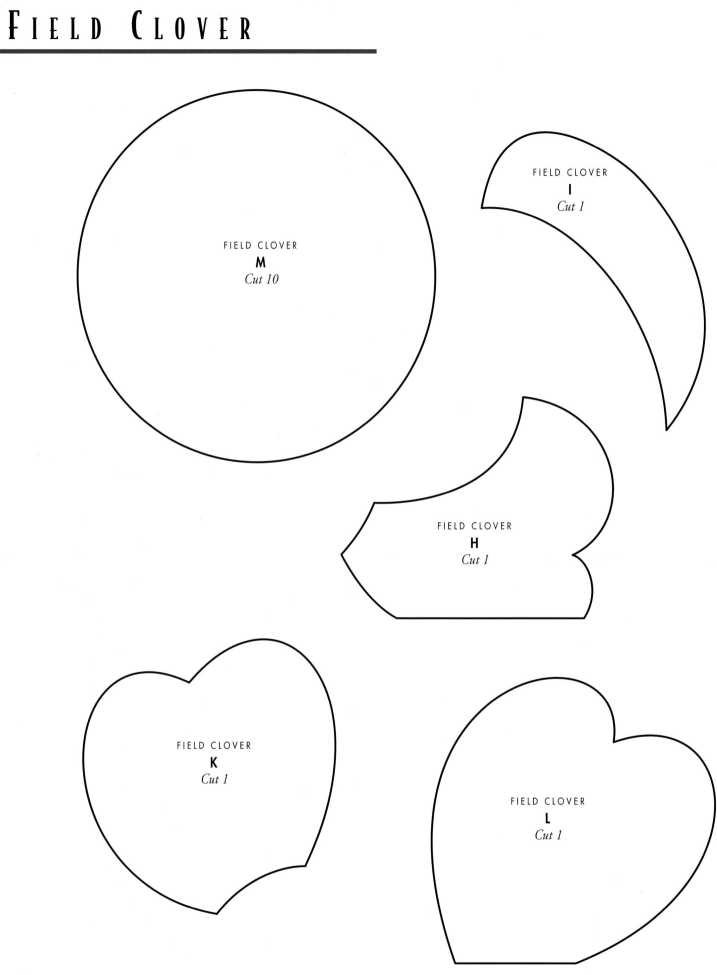

FIELD CLOVER
M
Cut 10

FIELD CLOVER
I
Cut 1

FIELD CLOVER
H
Cut 1

FIELD CLOVER
K
Cut 1

FIELD CLOVER
L
Cut 1

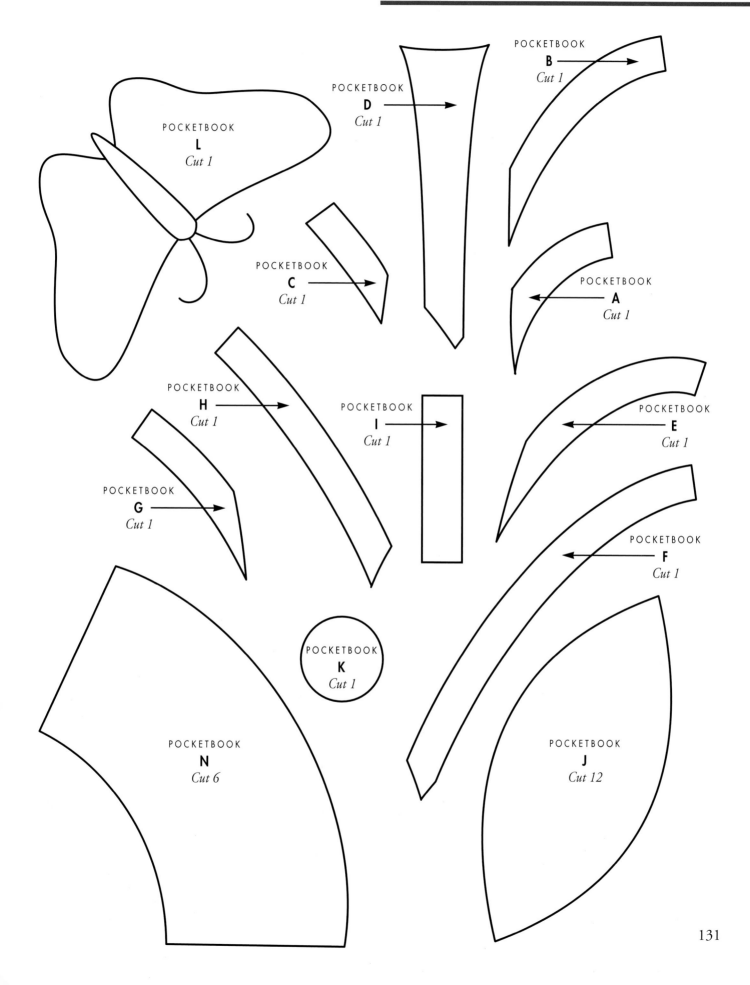

POCKETBOOK
L
Cut 1

POCKETBOOK
D
Cut 1

POCKETBOOK
B
Cut 1

POCKETBOOK
C
Cut 1

POCKETBOOK
A
Cut 1

POCKETBOOK
H
Cut 1

POCKETBOOK
I
Cut 1

POCKETBOOK
E
Cut 1

POCKETBOOK
G
Cut 1

POCKETBOOK
F
Cut 1

POCKETBOOK
K
Cut 1

POCKETBOOK
N
Cut 6

POCKETBOOK
J
Cut 12

POCKETBOOK

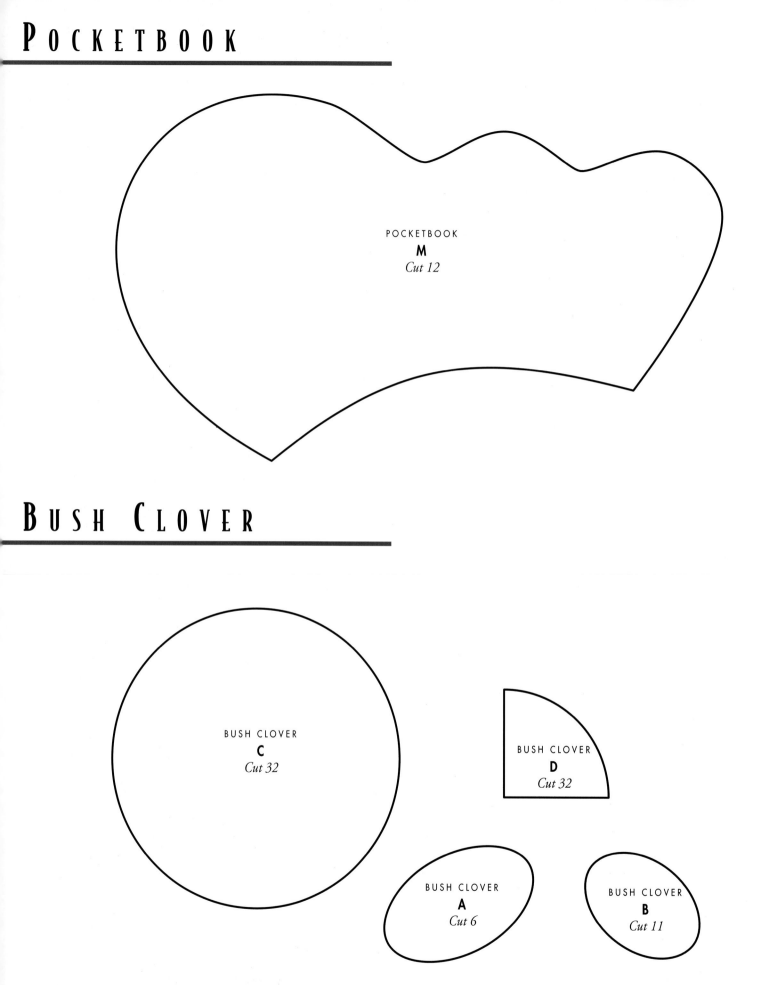

POCKETBOOK
M
Cut 12

BUSH CLOVER

BUSH CLOVER
C
Cut 32

BUSH CLOVER
D
Cut 32

BUSH CLOVER
A
Cut 6

BUSH CLOVER
B
Cut 11

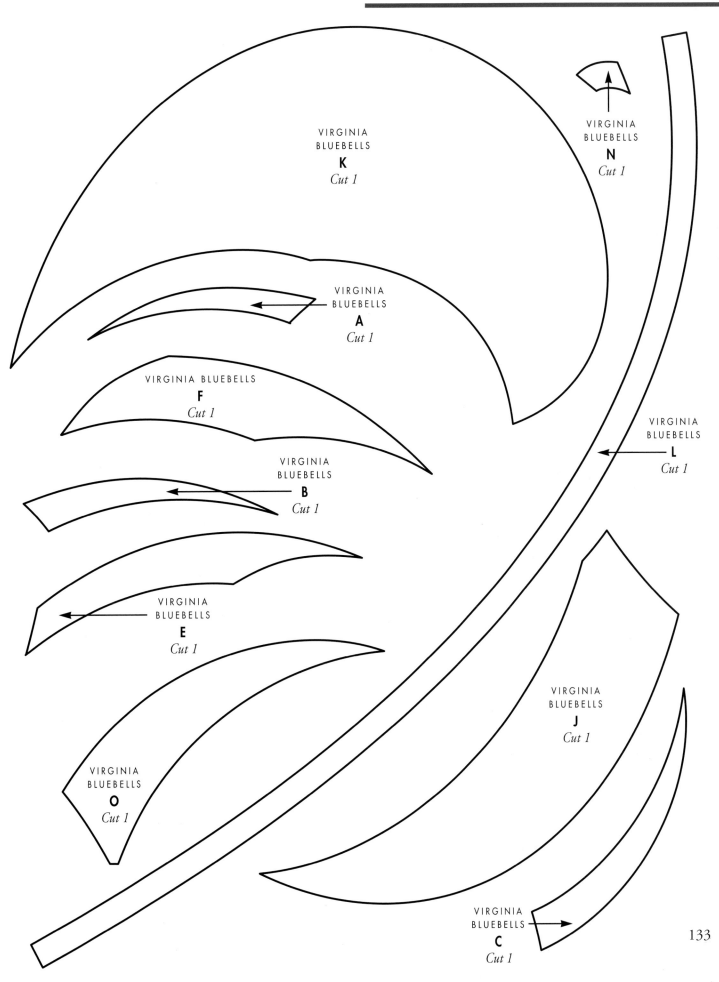

VIRGINIA
BLUEBELLS

K

Cut 1

VIRGINIA
BLUEBELLS

N

Cut 1

VIRGINIA
BLUEBELLS

A

Cut 1

VIRGINIA BLUEBELLS

F

Cut 1

VIRGINIA
BLUEBELLS

B

Cut 1

VIRGINIA
BLUEBELLS

L

Cut 1

VIRGINIA
BLUEBELLS

E

Cut 1

VIRGINIA
BLUEBELLS

J

Cut 1

VIRGINIA
BLUEBELLS

O

Cut 1

VIRGINIA
BLUEBELLS

C

Cut 1

133

VIRGINIA BLUEBELLS

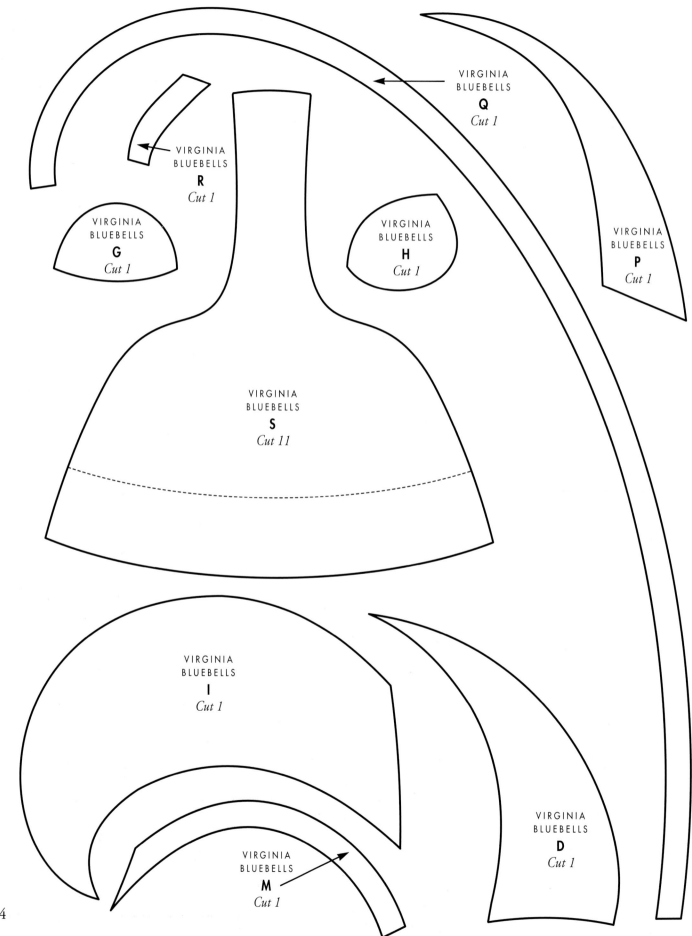

VIRGINIA
BLUEBELLS
Q
Cut 1

VIRGINIA
BLUEBELLS
R
Cut 1

VIRGINIA
BLUEBELLS
G
Cut 1

VIRGINIA
BLUEBELLS
H
Cut 1

VIRGINIA
BLUEBELLS
P
Cut 1

VIRGINIA
BLUEBELLS
S
Cut 11

VIRGINIA
BLUEBELLS
I
Cut 1

VIRGINIA
BLUEBELLS
D
Cut 1

VIRGINIA
BLUEBELLS
M
Cut 1

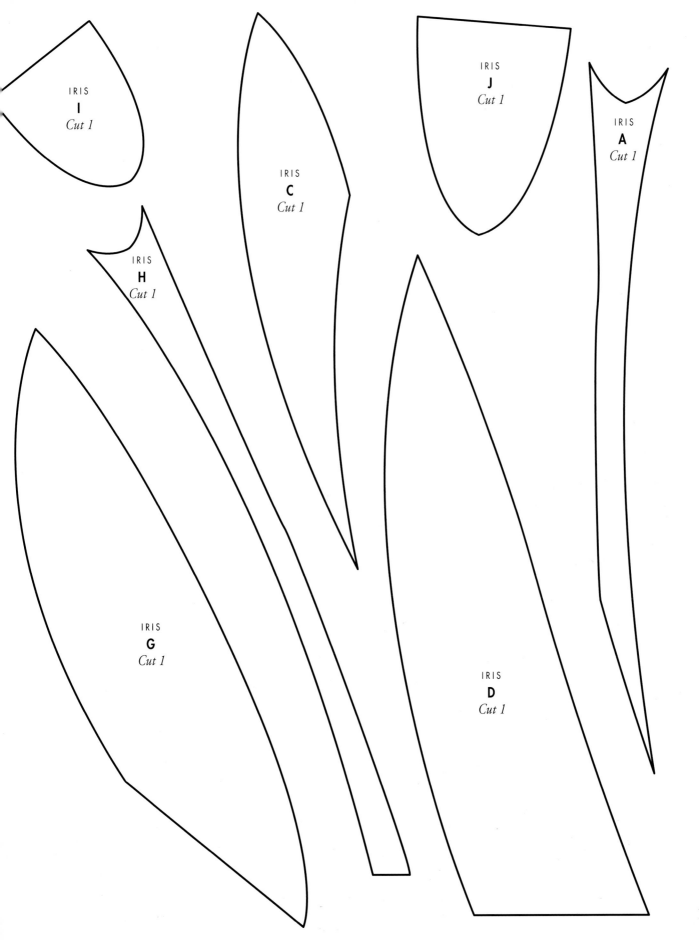

IRIS
I
Cut 1

IRIS
J
Cut 1

IRIS
A
Cut 1

IRIS
C
Cut 1

IRIS
H
Cut 1

IRIS
G
Cut 1

IRIS
D
Cut 1

Iris

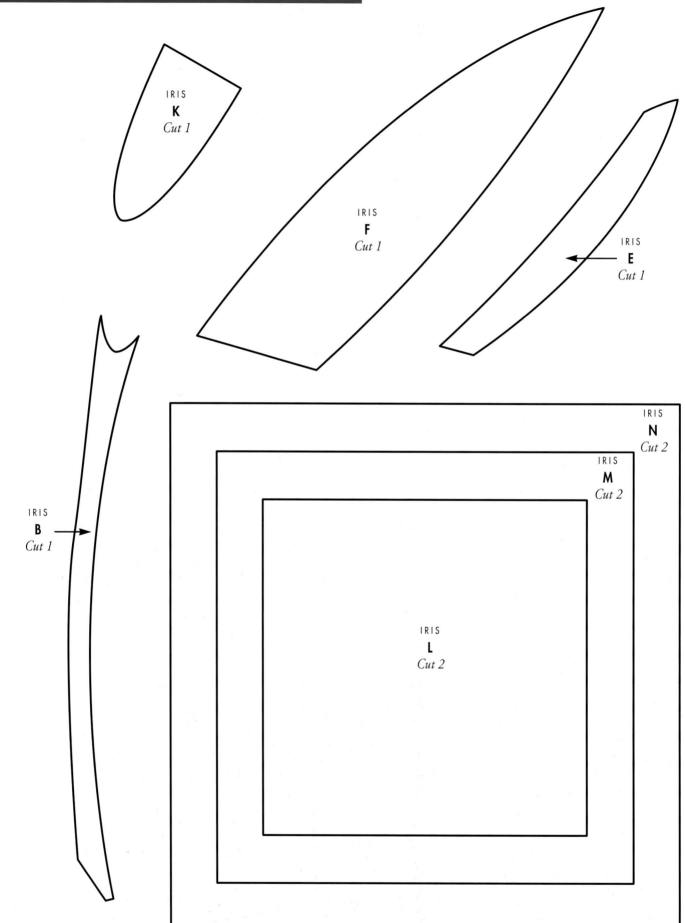

IRIS
K
Cut 1

IRIS
F
Cut 1

IRIS
E
Cut 1

IRIS
N
Cut 2

IRIS
M
Cut 2

IRIS
L
Cut 2

IRIS
B
Cut 1

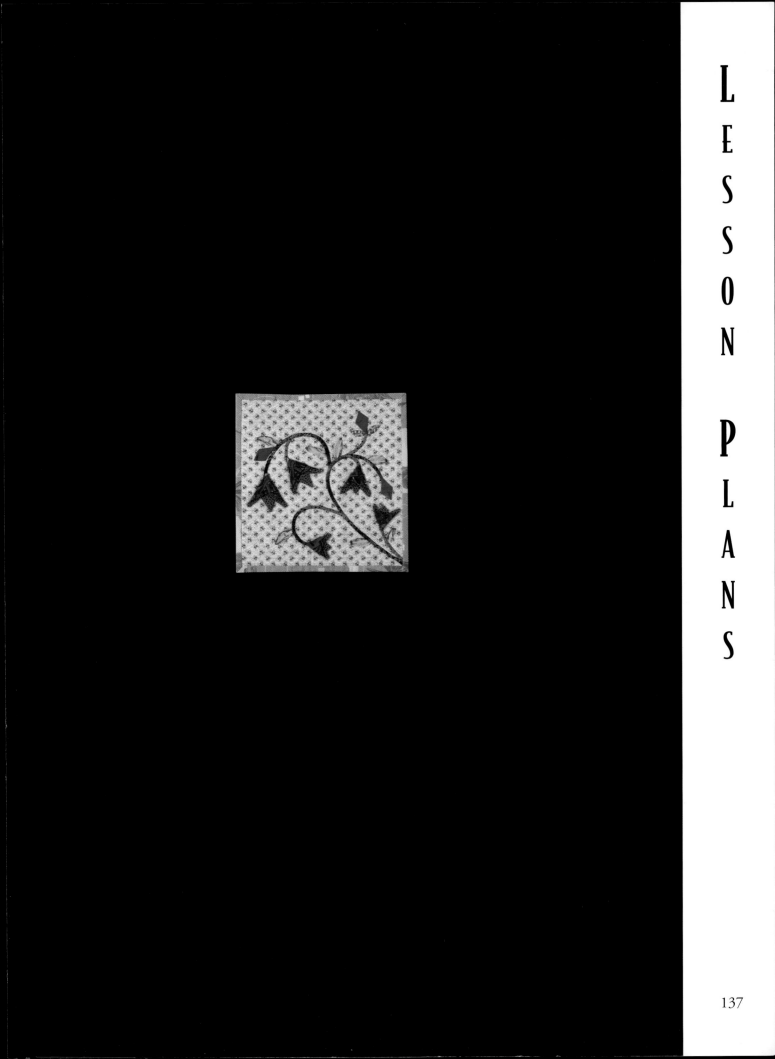

LESSON PLANS

Supply List for Each Workshop

- ❖ Sewing, quilting, and embroidery needles
- ❖ Sewing, quilting, and embroidery thread
- ❖ Straight pins
- ❖ Paper and fabric scissors
- ❖ Tracing paper
- ❖ Template plastic
- ❖ Ruler
- ❖ Pencil

- ❖ Colored pencils
- ❖ Thimble
- ❖ Fabric marker (or pencil)
- ❖ White drawing paper
- ❖ Fabric for the quilt top
- ❖ Backing fabric
- ❖ Batting
- ❖ Notebook

Suggestions for a One-Day Workshop Making a Simple Block: Fuchsia
(For Beginning and Intermediate Quilters)

During this sample lesson, students will make one of the easier blocks in this book. The process includes learning and practicing a method of appliqué and looking at color and pattern in fabrics in a new way. It also introduces the student to fabric folding or origami for three-dimensional effects.

First Hour

Give each student one or more photocopies of the diagram for the Fuchsia block (page 10). Discuss color selection and placement in the block: contrast of light and dark colors, texture, movement, and use of bold fabric and large design. Instruct students to experiment with color by coloring their photocopies and then making their final choices on colors they will use. As well as choosing fabric colors, choose a color for the embroidery thread to be used on the sashiko pattern. The color of the thread should stand out against the fabric. If you have time, give students some fabric scraps to practice folding fabric to create new shapes.

Second Hour

Students select background fabric and cut out the background square, following the length-wise grain or the print of the fabric pattern. Following the diagram on page 10, students lightly draw the outlines of the pattern onto the fabric using a pencil or fabric marker. Next, students trace the sashiko pattern from page 77 onto the fabric. After basting a piece of batting to the back of the background square, students complete the sashiko, stitching through the batting in even stitches.

Third Hour

After discussing the type of fabric to be used for the project, students select the fabrics that they will need to match their color sketches as closely as possible. They cut all the fabric pieces using the templates, following the lengthwise grain or the print of the fabric patterns. To complete the background square, students pin and appliqué the leaves and the buds, following the instructions on page 10.

Fourth and Fifth Hours

Students make the flowers following the instructions on page 11. Have students practice the origami folds on scrap fabric before making their flowers. Advise the students to make one complete flower first before starting on the others so that they have a model to follow. Students sew the completed flowers in position onto the background square.

Sixth Hour

After completing the block top, students join the top, batting, and quilt backing with basting stitches. If they do not wish the quilting to interfere with the sashiko design, students should quilt following the seamlines.

Suggestions for an Extended Classroom Schedule
Making a More Complex Design: Poppy Block or Quilt
(For intermediate and advanced quilters)

These are ideas to be incorporated into a course for teaching experienced quilters how to refine their appliqué skills and to gain further confidence in using fabric folding to create three-dimensional designs. The course is based on a design that includes many curved seams. More difficult than straight seams, these offer more design possibilities. It also includes suggestions for those who wish to encourage students to create their own three-dimensional designs. Feel free to use these ideas along with your own teaching experience to modify the course as you wish.

Using the Poppy design on page 34, begin by instructing students to make the block following the instructions and the procedure outlined in the earlier lesson. Students may make and finish just one block or the full quilt.

Demonstrate the appliqué technique used in this design. You may also wish to demonstrate other techniques for piecing curved seams and other forms of appliqué.

Discuss the use of color in the project–Kumiko has made wonderful use of contrasting colors in Poppy. Have students experiment with different colors and see how the image changes. Try out different colors of embroidery thread for the sashiko patterns, too.

To encourage creativity, demonstrate how new flower designs can be drawn. Students who have completed the Poppy block may wish to progress toward creating their own Poppy designs. Instruct students to make freehand drawings for a new Poppy block, moving the stems, leaves, and flowers around the block to create an entirely different image. Use colored pencils to experiment with different colors.

Students who have created new designs can form small groups and share their ideas. Conduct an open discussion about the pros and cons of each design.